# HERO
## OF WEST IRVINGTON PLACE

by

Doris Auger Davis

First Printing 2011
Printed in the United States of America

ISBN 978-0966598612

D.A. Davis, Publisher
P.O. Box 441252
Aurora, Colorado 80044-1252

BOOKS BY
Doris Auger Davis

**Flower of the Nile**

Copyright © 1998 by Doris Auger Davis
Library of Congress in Publication Data
First Printing 1998
ISBN 978-0966598612
Printed in the United States of America

FOR EDITH

As the younger daughter of a loving family, it was my good fortune to have had the companionship and leadership of my older sister. She remained my best and truest friend all
of her life.

If love could be captured in a single word,
it would surely be called
EDITH.

*The Author*

MANY GRATEFUL THANKS TO MY HUSBAND HENRY AND MY DAUGHTER JENNY FOR THEIR HELP IN PROOFREADING

# FORWARD

This is a true story. A few names have been shortened for reasons of privacy. Some of it is remembered by the author as a young child. A vivid memory sometimes fails to recall all details but every effort has been made to help the reader see through those innocent eyes of yesteryear.

The author has done extensive research to help explain the circumstances affecting many Americans at a very difficult time in our country's history.

As a Denver, Colorado native, the author has attempted to describe places and events associated with the "Mile High City" and the colorful state of which it is the capitol.

The main reason for writing this story is to memorialize a remarkable man who was born into poverty then pulled himself up by sheer will and determination to become a labor leader and spokesman for those who could not speak for themselves.

This is the account of an ordinary working man and his family and friends who lived through the Great Depression during the early 1930s.

It is the story of a hero. There are all kinds of heroes – heroes of war, heroes of medicine, heroes of love, to name a few. The title of hero is usually reserved for a person distinguished for valor, fortitude, or bold enterprise. Words like courage, nobility, sacrifice, and selfless commitment to a great cause are reserved for the few who have earned the right to be singled out for such acclaim.

Perhaps you can forgive the author for being so proud to be the daughter of loving and devoted parents who, against all odds, did their best to raise a family, contribute to their community, and make the world a better place because they passed this way.

James W. Shirley never knew he was a hero, but to his family and to those he served in the struggle to improve their lives through organized labor, he became the

HERO OF WEST IRVINGTON PLACE.

# CONTENTS

# PICTURES

# PREFACE
## DENVER, COLORADO

Denver's exciting history began during the gold and silver rush of the 1850s. An article from The Denver Post reported:

*In November 1858, Colorado was still part of Kansas Territory, where the governor was James W. Denver. A group of Kansan prospectors and merchants, some of whom were officials appointed by the governor, went looking for gold and to settle the area that eventually became Denver. They decided to name the site at the confluence of Cherry Creek and the South Platte River in honor of the Kansas governor, possibly to gain favor. While the group was en route, the governor had resigned, but the name of the town stayed the same.*

By 1860, Denver was a booming mining and cattle camp. Gunslingers, con men, prospectors, and gamblers roamed the dirt streets. The sound of their heels supporting high leather boots thumped along and their spurs clinked loudly as they made their way down the wooden sidewalks. And by 1870 Larimer Street was the center for saloons, gambling halls, and brothels. Many were hunting for their fortune in gold that would enable them to acquire property and social status. Greed showed its ugly head many times. Some men were never satisfied. The "Cow Town" grew rapidly.

The United States Mint opened in Denver in 1863 to melt gold dust and nuggets into gold bars.

Transportation was of great importance to the growing city of

Denver. The first Denver Pacific train arrived in the city on June 24, 1870. The Union Pacific had done the original track work which was reported as "not remarkably even." There was a celebration as tracks of the Kansas Pacific Railway arrived from Kansas City and St. Louis two months later.

The streetcar system began with a horse-drawn trolley from 7th and Larimer Streets to 27th and Champa Streets in 1871.

By 1881, the city was home to the massive Union Station at the foot of 17th Street, abode for many trains each day. An arch, which cost $22,000, weighing 70 tons and rising 50 feet at its highest point, welcomed visitors entering Denver streets. The reverse of the arch bade "Mitzpah" ("farewell" in Hebrew) to those leaving the city. (The arch was demolished in 1931 after officials deemed it a traffic hazard.)

Completion of the railroad station spurred the construction of other buildings nearby. Banks, hotels, and office buildings began to appear.

By 1927, Denver Tramway trolleys had reached out to the new suburbs of Congress Park, Curtis Park, Montclair, Cherry Creek, Englewood, and Littleton. Permanent tracks were installed in the middle of the streets. Streetcars gathered electric current from an overhead wire and transmitted it to the motor. It was a fun prank for young boys to run out to the slowing trolley and pull the connecting rod off. The driver had to get off and reattach it, much to his dismay. Ah, the energy of youth!

Other forms of transportation changed drastically over the years reducing the need for passenger trains and trolleys. Buses replaced the trolleys in 1950.

The air age for Denver began in 1929 with the building of Denver Municipal Airport (later Stapleton Airfield). It was located "far out on the plains" east of downtown Denver. It closed in 1995 to make way for Denver International Airport (DIA) much farther out of town. The facility lived up to its press releases. A failed baggage system delayed its opening for 16 months; DIA saw its first planes arrive on May 15, 1995. The airport was reported as the 11th busiest in the world in the early 2000s. The old Stapleton site was redeveloped for housing and commerce.

Redevelopment of Union Station and the revival of the trolley system, known in 2009 as *FasTracks*, makes the depot a transportation hub for light-rail routes eventually stretching to Golden, Boulder, the southeast suburbs, and Denver International Airport.

Throughout the 19th and 20th centuries, Denver reinvented and recreated itself from a rough frontier town to a modern, sophisticated city with all the amenities one would expect to find. From sports to retail development, and from stockyards to exhibition centers, creative minds and city planners cooperated in their quest for status and pride. Construction workers found meaningful outlets for their skills and crafts as the city boomed.

Although many of the grandiose building projects of the time have been replaced by newer facilities, the need to appreciate and remember lingers on.

The Milwaukee Brewery opened in 1890 and was one of the first breweries in Colorado, with the oldest water wells in Denver. By 1900, it operated as the Tivoli-Union Brewery.

The modern and elegant Brown Palace Hotel opened in the upper downtown area in 1892 and began hosting a stream of notables, including President Theodore Roosevelt. The skylight atrium in the lobby was the first of its kind in America. It was also one of the first fireproof structures built with sandstone walls and a granite base.

The State Capitol building, completed in 1908, took twenty-two years to build. Henry C. Brown, builder of the Brown Palace Hotel, contributed ten acres of land for its construction. It was designed by architect Elijah C. Myers who was later dismissed from the project in 1889 to save money. Architect F.E. Edbrooke was then appointed as an advisory architect. It was he who suggested the 24-carat gold dome. The gold, which was donated by Colorado mining companies, has been re-gilded several times. Another interesting fact is that it was modeled after the United States Capitol in Washington, D.C., but the stately Colorado Capitol is unique in the 24-carat gold leaf covering. The many steps to the top reveals a wonderful view of the famous and majestic Rocky Mountains. On the 15th step from the street below, a plaque identifies the elevation as exactly one mile above sea level.

The Denver City and County Building opened in 1932 and boasted of a gold eagle and carillon clock tower atop the building.

Amid much fanfare, the Daniels and Fisher Tower was hailed as Denver's tallest structure when it opened in 1938. The 372-foot tower, modeled in the campanile style of St. Mark's in Venice, Italy was part of a very elite department store.

The old Stockyard Stadium which had hosted the National Western Stock Show was enlarged and renamed the Denver Coliseum in 1952 before a crowd of 10,000. The cost was 2.3 million dollars. The first show at the Coliseum was *Sonja Henie's 1952 Ice Revue*. (The author was privileged to attend and appreciate the skills of such a wonderful artist on ice.)

Zeckendorf Plaza at 16th Street near Broadway was built in 1958. It included a hotel, department store, and ice skating rink. (It was partially demolished in 1996 as part of an expansion of the Adam's Mark Hotel.)

In 1969, Currigan Exhibition Hall opened as the precursor to the Colorado Convention Center. It was a unique structure in that the panels were bolted together rather than welded. Its unusual design allowed a clear span of 120 feet which, at that time, was said to be the largest span in the nation without columns. (It was demolished in the early 2000s.)

Denver was home to many movie theatres. The Mayan and Webber are described later in the book for personal reasons. Some others that were popular were the Orpheum, Vogue, Bluebird, Aladdin, Rialto, Oriental, Broadway, Tabor, and Paramount.

The author hopes that the inclusion of these few selected facts and events about Denver will stimulate the reader to delve more deeply into the history of Denver and the state of Colorado.

# PREFACE
## LABOR MOVEMENT

Organized labor has often felt and been treated like an uninvited guest at a banquet hosted by the leaders of industry and commerce. For each gain in acceptance and equality there have been numerous setbacks. Violence has been commonplace on both sides of the table. This was especially true in the 19th and early 20th centuries. Labor's small gains through the years of World War I and the Roaring Twenties in a crusade for true acceptance was far from over. It would take an economic depression and a change of political climate to give labor a giant step forward.

A brief look at the early history of the American labor movement might prove helpful in understanding the struggles faced by workers. As unions became stronger, employers attempted to destroy their effectiveness by hiring non-union workers (commonly called "scabs") and by appealing to the courts to declare labor organization illegal. The fight against unions was carried through the courts in Philadelphia, New York, and Pittsburgh between 1806 and 1814. Unions were persecuted as "conspiracies in restraint of trade" under an old English Common Law doctrine that stated combinations of workmen wanting to raise wages could be regarded as a conspiracy against the public. Several unions were found guilty and fined. Some became bankrupt as a result and disbanded.

However, through the 1800's many unions were formed and new Federal laws were enacted. In 1886 the American Federation of Labor was organized at a convention in Columbus, Ohio as a successor to the Federation of Organized Trades and Labor Unions which had been organized in 1881. Also, the same year, the United Brotherhood of Carpenters and Joiners was organized.

Labor suffered a setback in 1886 in the aftermath of the Haymarket Riot and bombing in Chicago in which 4 workers and 7 police died. Eight anarchists were tried, found guilty, and hanged. Likewise, the violence of the Pullman Strike of 1894 did little to endear the union cause to many Americans.

The uneasy and hostile relationship between organized labor and corporate management simmered and frequently flared up in Colorado during this period. Hard rock miners and coal miners were prime candidates for unionization. As organized labor began to flex its muscles, corporate management stiffened its opposition. It seemed inevitable that a major confrontation was in the offing.

In 1913, the coal mining town of Ludlow, Colorado had a population of close to 1,000. The town had general stores, blacksmith stables, a church, three schools, a bakery, a dairy, and even a book and stationery store. This was a company town operated by the Colorado Fuel and Iron Company, owned John D. Rockefeller, that controlled workers by paying them in script instead of money. Script was redeemable only at the company stores. The coal miners worked in a dangerous occupation. Frequent deaths and accidents occurred. Workers toiled 10 to 12 hours a day in the mines and returned to company houses at the end of each shift. They had long sought better working conditions and union representation.

On September 23, 1913, a strike by the United Mine Workers of America began in Las Animas and Huerfano counties. An estimated 12,000 to 13,000 miners and their families, evicted from their company-owned homes, moved into tent cities where they suffered through a snowy Colorado winter. One such tent city was at Ludlow.

The mine owners responded to the strike by asking the State to deploy the Colorado Militia to maintain order. Shots rang out at Ludlow as the strikers went to collect their mail on October 7, 1913. Two days later, the strikers began digging cellars under their tents after hearing that mine guards had armed themselves with machine guns.

One of the most violent and tragic conflicts in the history of American Labor took place on Monday, April 20, 1914 and became etched in the conscience of American history as the *Ludlow Massacre*.

The day was a long one. There was a fierce battle between units of the Colorado National Guard and striking coal mine workers. Women and children ran as fast as they could, dodging the bullets that were fired at them by the guardsmen. An owner of a nearby ranch reported that he had witnessed four or five guardsmen methodically set a group of tents on fire. A Ludlow postmistress said she had seen the same scene from the depot yards. When she went to the colony site, she said she found it a deserted shambles of blackened tent poles, skeletal bedsteads, shards of pottery and glass, scorched floorboards, and charred clothing. She also found a friend wandering in a daze, unclear of the whereabouts of her children. Another acquaintance of hers was in a similar incoherent state. The women told her that their underground refuge had been in the second row of tents from the rear. It was not until Tuesday afternoon that an underground pit was uncovered exposing the thirteen bodies of: Patricia Valdez and her four children: Elvira, three months; Eulala, 8; Mary, 7; and Rudolph, 9. The pregnant Cedilano Costa and her children: Onafrio, 6 and Lucy, 4. The two Pedregon children: Gloria, 4 and Roderlo, 6. The three Petrucci children: Frank, six months; Lucy, 1 and Joe, 4.

Nearly a dozen others were killed during the melee, including women and children who were shot in cold blood as they ran from the burning tents.

In retaliation, vengeful miners burned several mines and camps in the area. It was another eight months before the strike ended in a stalemate.

The record shows that the 1913-14 strike was lost by the United Mine Workers, but in reality, it was won. It is true that the great strike was brought to an end by the organization before its objectives were achieved, but public opinion, which had been aroused as never before or since in an industrial dispute, battered down the gates of the coal operators and in the end, the miners and citizens of Colorado were the victors.

What happened at Ludlow produced the Industrial Relations Act of 1915, giving every worker in the State the right to strike. It brought the miners tangible gains in welfare, medical care, housing, recreation, and education. However, in no sense were the employees' representatives allowed powers of decision. It wasn't until 1933 that the Colorado Fuel and Iron Company (CFI) negotiated its first genuine collective-bargaining agreement with the United Mine Workers (UMW) and in 1935 the Wagner Act effectively outlawed the practice of company unions.

If the account seems biased in favor of labor in general and the coal miners in particular, we must remember that it deals with a period in our industrial history when the gun, the club, and the fist were often the sole methods of management and labor communication. The Colorado record of that decade is clear and substantiated, not once but many times by courts of record and the earnest findings of impartial and honest investigators.

A sober and respectful memorial of the Ludlow Massacre may be seen 17 miles north of Trinidad, Colorado off Interstate 25 at exit 27, approximately 200 miles south of Denver.

The mining towns of southern Colorado were not the only places where laborers met with hard times. Underpaid agricultural workers were often hidden from sight because of the isolation of their places of employment. One crop was especially vulnerable to exploitation - sugar beets.

Beet production was important in Denver and other parts of Colorado. It depended upon cheap hand labor. In the early 1930's, low wages and depressed conditions were not the sole reasons for poverty among sugar beet workers. Technological advancements led to replacement of many workers by machines. Children were forced to drop out of school at an early age in order to help support their families and a family would desperately contract to harvest a certain area for a specified wage, often barely enough to sustain one individual. Nearly all farm children over eight years of age worked in the fields, usually twelve hours a day. Families lived under almost unbelievable conditions. Some companies loaned tools and materials to the migrants to build their own homes in colonies on company land. Workers were to repay the loan through wage deduction installments. In reality, lower wages resulting from the Depression permitted only the barest subsistence and left little or no money for repayment of home loans.

When migrants refused to work for such low pay, all beet workers were excluded from relief rolls. Working conditions in the beet industry approached industrial slavery. The average worker earned $78 for the season, approximately one-quarter of the minimum amount needed to support a family of four.

During the latter 1930's, the problem of migrant labor gradually changed. In 1937, the American Federation of Labor (AFL) and the Congress of Industrial Organizations (CIO) organized 8,000 beet workers in Colorado. Although the CIO demanded better working conditions for its members, it failed to obtain any noteworthy results until 1940. In a series of labor hearings that year, the Department of Agriculture led the federal government to set a decent minimum wage for beet workers.

CHAPTER I

# FAMILY ROOTS

# FAMILY ROOTS

The high plains of northwest Kansas could be both nurturing and punishing to those brave souls who chose to settle there in the late 1800's. Bands of Indians were occasionally seen in the distance as they struggled to accept the steady encroachment of settlers from the south and east.

Small subsistence farms and a few larger farms began to occupy the land around the quaint settlement of Atwood. On one small farm, William James Shirley (b. 1875) and his wife, Cary Mae Gibson Shirley (b. 1885) worked tirelessly to till the soil and raise their family. William, or "Will" as he was known, had twin brothers Ed and Eb. Ed lived on a nearby farm with his wife, Minnie, and Eb lived in Wray, Colorado. A sister, Laura Nonkin, lived in Topeka, Kansas where her family owned a furniture store.

It was here on the rolling plains of Kansas that the hero of my story, James William Shirley, breathed his first breath on May 28, 1903. The old white farm house took on new life and energy as this hearty-lunged infant settled in with his proud parents and three-year-old sister, Orda.

On one of the neighboring farms, good friends of the Shirley family had unknowingly built their new home directly on the Kansas-Nebraska state line, much to their dismay. When a child was born in the house, the parents had to be careful as to which room was in Kansas and which one was in Nebraska. Since the court house was in nearby Atwood where the records of the births were kept, they would make sure that the birthing room was in Kansas. There were many jokes made about the problem as the family increased their brood, always making sure to use that special room.

Fortune did not always smile on the Shirleys. In spite of hard work, Will could not overcome the economic crisis gripping most of the west after 1893. He found it necessary to move his young family to a "soddy" nearby. Though not as comfortable as the house had been, the soddy was adequate for their needs. Claire, the youngest, was born in the soddy in 1908 and in later years, was reluctant to talk about the humble beginnings of the family. It is not known how long the family lived in the sod house or whether they were able to move back to the farmhouse during the remainder of their stay in Kansas.

Later years, when Will would reminisce about life on the farm, he would speak of seeing a few Indians strolling along in the distant hills. The family would laugh as if this was a ridiculous statement, just a figment of the imagination of an elderly man. They were wrong. There were roving Indians in western Kansas at that time.

Will had been fortunate in his life in that he had learned another trade while being a farmer. He became adept at plastering and cement work and had mastered artistic plastering which he taught to his son Jim. Little did he know that Jim would someday excel in artistic plastering to the point where he would be called upon to work on some of Denver's more impressive buildings and churches after the family's move to the big city.

There was a popular migration to the growing city of Denver of which Will was very aware. By 1913, it was evident that Cary Mae's health was failing. Each day she was becoming more disabled. The local doctor was unable to determine the nature of her

*Cary Mae Gibson and William James Shirley*

illness. After much thought and deliberation Will decided to move his family to Denver where possibly better medical attention would be available. Fifteen-year-old Orda, 12-year-old Jim, and 7-year-old Claire packed their meager belongings for the move to Colorado.

By the time the Shirley family arrived in Denver in 1915, the town had changed from the famous gold rush days of the 1800's. Their first residence was at 482 Pearl Street. It seemed an ideal location for Cary Mae with her health not improving. Will was hopeful that a Denver doctor could diagnose her problem. But it was the same sad story. The medical community could offer no explanation for her condition.

I can remember as a very small child, standing before my Grandmother Cary Mae, in a dimly lit room in the Pearl Street house, and marveling at the wheelchair with its large wheels in which she sat. I could not understand why I was not allowed to sit on her lap. In spite of my inclination to climb up and hug her, I kept my distance.

Life changed dramatically for the Shirley family in their new Denver home. After Cary Mae lost her battle for life, it was very difficult for the family to adjust with her absence. But as we all know, life must go on. She died in 1932 at the age of 47. When I was older and after her death, Daddy explained to me that anything, even something as light as a piece of paper placed on her lap would cause her great discomfort. My Aunt Orda and Aunt Claire more than made up for the lack of affection unintentionally denied by my grandmother.

My Aunt Orda was not an attractive woman by most standards, with a rather pronounced nose that seemed to accentuate her long face. Her dark hair was not as well kept as was her attractive sister Claire's. But she had a heart of gold and a sharp mind which she filled with facts from newspapers, magazines, books, and radio. She was a delightful conversationalist. In later years when she lived in Fontana, California, we would call each other on the telephone to discuss current events. My favorite was politics. Since we were of the same political party, it made for a very pleasant outlet - for both of us. Also, she never forgot to remember my sister Edith and me with a little gift on special occasions. When she was employed at Montgomery Ward as a comptometer operator, I recall receiving a row of small bottles filled with different perfume scents, encased in a container that had a tiny lock and key. What a memorable gift from a very thoughtful Aunt Orda.

While living at the Pearl Street address, Aunt Orda attended business school and excelled in learning the operation of a variety of business machines. The doors were always open for employment in the business field and compensation was very substantial. She married and was widowed twice, but never had any children. Her first marriage was to "Nick," short for Nickelson. He worked in construction as a "Powder Monkey" - one who plants dynamite in drilled rock to make way for new tunnels and roads. It was dangerous work but fortunately paid well. After his death she remarried but her second husband also died. She never married again but enjoyed the company of her beloved dogs. Her last home in Fontana was where she and the dogs enjoyed retirement among an orchard of fruit trees and a small garden.

Aunt Claire, the younger of the two sisters, had been blessed by nature with beautiful blond hair which she kept coiffured in the style of a fashion model. Light blue eyes and a charming dimple in her chin made her the envy of other girls in her neighborhood. She was gifted with an operatic voice and some skills as a dancer. Her very lovely voice landed her in some of Denver's major stage productions. In *Rio Rita* sponsored by Father Bozetti, she had the lead role.

By this time the family had moved to 628 South Ogden Street near Washington Park. It was called a *double* residence and Will had purchased it so the family could live on one side (the south side of the duplex) while the other side could be rented.

Aunt Claire and Paul Wood were sweethearts when they attended South High School in Denver. They both graduated in 1924, the first graduating class in the new building and were married afterwards in 1933. They moved to Fort Collins, Colorado and opened a florist shop on Main Street and named it *Wood's Florist Shop*. Aunt Claire continued her singing and dancing career. She taught dancing at one time and sang at many events and also worked alongside her husband in the florist shop. After the birth of their son David, the proud parents devoted their lives to this precious gift. David became a lawyer in Fort Collins and later served for a period as the Assistant District Attorney in Larimer County. Aunt Claire and Uncle Paul owned and operated the *Wood's Florist Shop* for fifty years. In 2008, new owners celebrated the 75th anniversary of the shop, now at a different location.

I can still remember Aunt Claire practicing her voice scales while standing and playing notes on the piano. She had shown Edith and me the gorgeous head piece that she was to wear for her part in Rio Rita. Afterwards, she gave us this and many of her other costumes from her performances. She was always so kind and generous all of her life. Sometime later when Edith and I decided that we would have an amateur production of our own, we used those costumes that Aunt Claire had given to us. Our theatrical career began at a later time when our family lived in the home on South Columbine Street. This house had a large basement which was ideal for childhood theatrical productions - so Edith and I thought. I was about ten years old and Edith was eleven. All of the neighborhood children were notified of our first show. They were delighted to attend and had to pay a penny at the basement door for a choice seat - mostly on the hard cement floor. It was a sold-out crowd!

This was before the room had been plastered and there was still a large opening leading into the furnace room. From that opening we made our grandiose entrances to our awaiting audience. Behind the furnace room was our dressing room. Since the costumes were far too large for us, keeping them on was at times quite challenging. I remember well on one occasion during one of my spirited performances, with the phonograph blaring, that my mother came down the basement stairs just as the upper part of my costume slid to my waist. I did not have on nor did I own a bra. The audience, both male and female, clapped and clapped - especially the young boys. This could possibly have been the forerunner of *Hooters* which became so popular many, many years later. My mother was so upset that the production ended quickly as she escorted the large audience up the stairs and out the back door. That was the end of our chances to Broadway careers. Neighborhood kids - mostly males - wanted to know when we would be having another show. Later that evening, when Daddy returned home from work, Mother filled him in with all of the details of the busy day. As Mother explained the costume event he just grinned. There was also a twinkle in his eyes.

In 1920, Jim Shirley's father Will (or "Pa" as Jim called him) recognized that his 17-year-old son had the physical characteristics and drive necessary to make a name for himself in the ring as a boxer.

So, let my story continue...

## CHAPTER II

# THE FIGHTER

*Jim Shirley, age 17, 1920*

# THE FIGHTER

The sign over the door read *QUINCY'S GYM*. Will Shirley and seventeen-year-old Jim entered the large door with eager anticipation. Neither of them was fully prepared for the new world opening up to them.

In later years when Jim related to his family his experiences in the boxing world, he would nostalgically recall that first mystifying day that changed his life and taught him the value of hard work, skill, and dogged determination in pursuit of one's goals.

Upon entering the dimly-lit, smoke-filled gym the odor of human perspiration permeated the atmosphere. Men and boys were crowded around the center of the room where an announcement was being made.

"Boxing isn't a game, it's an art," a slightly bald and somewhat paunchy trainer was explaining as he extolled the ancient sport of pugilism to his audience. "If you are going to survive in the ring you will soon learn that it takes more than strength and brute force to be a success in this business." He continued, "It's my job to teach you to bob and weave, duck and dance, and make your opponent miss more than he hits."

In the center of the small ring a sparring partner awaited the anxious boys as they climbed through the ropes and onto the canvas-covered floor.

Jim Shirley was larger and heavier than some of the eager students and was an obvious candidate to join the ranks of the heavyweights. As each boy took his turn with the sparring partner the trainer kept shouting, "Dance! Dance! Dance! if you don't want your nose busted! Keep those gloves up and make him miss!"

Each day became more grueling as the instruction intensified. The sparring partners seemed to grow in size and strength with every punch of the tight leather gloves. Jim's body ached in places he didn't know existed. But as each day ended he knew he was stronger and better than the day before. He was determined to become a champion.

Pa (Will) was always pushing him harder and harder.

Jim was bright and hard-working and became an excellent student of his trainers. At that time, formal public education ended with the 8th grade and one could become a teacher if they could pass the educational tests required for the job. Many of the boxing trainees did not have Jim's level of education nor a desire to advance academically. Jim laughingly bragged that he actually had "advanced" education because he felt his 8th grade teacher was so attractive that he repeated the course simply to be near her.

Students in the 19th and early 20 centuries had few options for continuing their education. Attending college was not possible for many. Learning a trade was the normal route to success and Jim was always grateful for his knowledge of the plastering trade if his boxing career did not work out.

Even as Jim applied himself to boxing, he continued to devour books on history, geography, mathematics, and the arts. This thirst for knowledge continued throughout his life. Jim's pretty 8th grade teacher would have been proud of the impact she had on him and his desire for knowledge.

By 1920 Jim - under the watchful eye of Pa - began to be noticed in the boxing community. Members of the sports media also recognized the potential of this attractive and charismatic newcomer. His work ethic at the Quincy Gym was impressive.

Articles from *The Denver Post* gave some encouraging reports:

*There are a couple of fellows working out at the Quincy Gym who may someday be strong contenders for heavyweight honors in the boxing game. They are Jim Shirley, 17 years old and weighs 180 pounds, and Pete Diehl, 23 years old, who weighs 175 pounds. They are ambitious to become efficient with their mitts. Both say that if they are capable of handling themselves they will take a whirl at the boxing game.*

Another article titled:

***HE'S BLACK AND BLUE***

*Over at the Quincy gym we found a healthy crowd working out under the watchful eye of Joe 'Wop' Flynn and Lee Warner. Lee didn't have his gym togs on. He was watching the lads, for he said his body was black and blue from the thumping the amateurs had given him during the past week while he was showing them a few tricks of the trade.*

Additional reports:

*The Denver Post* gave its sports readers more information as follows:

*At the Quincy there's one lad of whom much is expected. He is a middleweight named Jim Shirley, a well-built chap of pleasing appearance and manners and a dead game scrapper.*

*It's the same at the nine or ten other clubs where the simon purists are working out, but time forbids going the entire rounds.*

An "Elks Smoker" took place in 1921 at the Elk's home in Sterling, Colorado. The following appeared in *The Denver Post*:

*FERGUSON AND SHIRLEY FIGHT TO BE REAL ONE*

*The main topic of conversation among the local sports is the coming battle between Jim Shirley, Colorado's heavyweight champion, and Mose Ferguson, the Julesburg heavyweight, which takes place at the Elk's home in Sterling January 25.*

Also, an interesting article with a picture of Jim Shirley and Mose Ferguson, each in their fighting stance and is described BY CAL:

*If you want to find any old time boxer, boxing fan, cow-puncher, cattleman, professional man or the like tomorrow night it will be a good place to look him over at the Elk's home in Sterling, where he will be seen... show ever staged in northern Colorado.*

*You will see wise managers and pugs who appear to have more business than the average broker. You will see some bird motion another aside to a dark corner for a private conference; they whisper strange things to each other's ear. They nod and wink after the fashion of the wise guy. They slip each other bits of scribbled paper, notes, tips and a lot of inside stuff.*

*The pugs and managers are herded into a small room like so many cattle. They are admitted in bunches where they are given a cross examination. There is usually a bunch outside the door at the home, storming the door and waiting for some one to slip them an Anny Oakley.*

*The athletes stand around while their trainers puff huge clouds of smoke into their faces and tell them how they should breathe a lot of*

(By E. E. OVERHOLT.)

Dig up the old memorandum book and prepare to set down some records under the heading of "Amateur Boxing and Wrestling," for—

Records began to tumble at the Denver Athletic club last evening long before Jack Keene, heavyweight, took a series of tumbles in the opening boxing bout on the long card. Mr. Jim Shirley knocked Jack on the chin so often and so enthusiastically that Jack sat down hard and frequently. At the finish Jack was as bad off as the shipping board—he was all at sea—and they dragged him away to make room for others.

## Jimmy Shirley, Heavyweight Star of the Quincy String, Is Class of Heavyweights That Have Shown Their Wares to Date—Campbell a Hard Hitter

By HARRY D. HOFFMAN

Jimmy Shirley, blonde haired pride of the Quincy gym, was a step nearer the amateur heavyweight title, when he knocked out Charley Miller of the Tramway club in three rounds, at the D. A. C. tourney last night.

Shirley is the class of the heavyweights who have shown their wares at the big biff classic. He appears to have an excellent chance of copping the heavyweight title and a gold watch. However, there are many more tough birds for Jimmy to dispose of and it's a bit early to make predictions. The lad's work last night stood out.

He was the aggressor thruout and kept using a straight left to Miller's face that carried power behind it. In each of the three rounds he scored knockdowns and had his man punch drunk at the finish. Shirley is a two-handed fighter and can shoot a lightning-like right, but withal it looks as if his left is his big gun, for he jarred Miller every time he landed with his portside.

*Articles of The Denver Post 1920*
*(by E.E. Overholt)*

### SHIRLEY WINS

The first boxing bout was between Jimmy Shirley of the Quincy gym and Jack Keene of Knorr's stable. Keene had it on Shirley in regards to weight but Jimmy proved the better boxer and the hardest puncher. He put Keene down on the canvas in the first stanza, repeated in the second and sent him out for keeps in the third. Watch this boy Shirley; he looks good to us.

Jimmy Shirley, Quincy, and Charles Miller, Tramway, semi-finalists in the heavyweight class, furnished one of the real battles of the evening. Early in the opening round Shirley showed that he had a good left, as well as an equally good right, and it wasn't long before he had Miller in a bad way. He left-jabbed the Tramway man repeatedly, but Miller always came back for more, landing a number of heavy thumps himself. Miller went down in the second from a volley of lefts and again in the third. He was practically out on his feet just before the bell, but too game to quit. The bout was Shirley's easily.

*fresh air and how they ought to train for this and that fighter... coming bout. Each one has been donning the gloves daily and stepping off five or six fast rounds after which they have been receiving a brisk rub down. They are leaving nothing undone in the way of getting into the best of shape for their coming fray.*

*Both have been wanting to settle their little dispute for some time and they have decided to settle it in a gentlemanly manner in the roped area. No matter who wins, they have both agreed to bury the hatchet immediately after the battle and become best of friends.*

Another article regarding the Jim Shirley-Mose Ferguson fight from *The Denver Post*:

*Swell dressers, near champions, preliminary boys and the down-and-out stand and chat. A big fellow with a rare design of cauliflower ears, a nose flat against his face and a brow that almost covers his eyes, might be seen talking to some prominent banker. They all mix up for a good time at the Elk's smoker. Many old celebrities will be on hand.*

*Should Mose Ferguson, the Julesburg heavyweight, win the bout with Jim Shirley, he will be in line for some important matches in the future. Once the gong sounds after Mose has crawled into the ring, the fireworks start. He never gives his opponent a minute's rest. This has been the history of his battles in the past.*

*Mose Ferguson weighed in at 180 pounds, and Jim Shirley of Denver at 175 for the main event. Both proved to be youngsters. Shirley is but 18 years old and Ferguson around 20. Shirley is a well built chap, while Ferguson was angular, with an advantage of several inches in his reach. The Julesburg lad strode about the ring in his robe and grinned at his*

# THEY'LL ALL BE AT THE RING AT THE ELKS' SMOKER TOMORROW

(BY CAL.)

If you want to find any old time boxer, boxing fan, cow-puncher, cattleman, professional man or the like tomorrow night, it will be a good place to look him over at the Elks' home in Sterling, where he will be seen show ever staged in northern Colorado.

You will see wise managers and pugs who appear to have more business than the average broker. You will see some bird motion another aside to a dark corner for a private conference; they whisper strange things in each other's ear. They nod and wink after the fashion of the wise guy. They slip each other bits of scribbled paper, notes, tips and a lot of inside stuff.

The pugs and managers are herded into a small room like so many cattle. They are admitted in bunches where they are given a cross examination. There is usually a bunch outside the door at the home, storming the door and waiting for some one to slip them an Anny Oakley.

The athletes stand around while their trainers puff huge clouds of smoke into their faces and tell them how they should breathe a lot of fresh air and how they ought to train for this and that fighter.

coming bout. Each one has been donning the gloves daily and stepping off five or six fast rounds after which they have been receiving a brisk rub down. They are leaving nothing undone in the way of getting into the best of shape for their coming fray.

Both have been wanting to settle their little dispute for some time and they have decided to settle it in a gentlemanly manner in the roped arena. No matter who wins, they have both agreed to bury the hatchet immediately after the battle and become the best of friends.

MOSE FERGUSON

JIM SHIRLEY

*The Denver Post 1921*

*supporters as they cheered him on, for there were many Julesburg fans in the assembly. Shirley sat quietly in his corner. It was announced that they would go eight rounds. Cal Cheairs was the mediator.*

*Ferguson opened up by doing a hornpipe around the ring, which added nothing to the confidence that was reposed in him, because there were any number of men present who could dance better than he. Shirley went about his work more cautiously. Ferguson, by reason of his long reach, kept Shirley at arms length during the first round, and while each placed blows, there were no signs on a decided advantage for either.*

**Experience Proves Value** - *The second round also was even; in the third Shirley began to display his better defense and was coming inside the radius of Ferguson's arm. In the clinches he came off to the advantage. In the fourth he further proved his better experience, landing his blows at the spot at which they were aimed. In the fifth Shirley reached Ferguson's nose, to bring the claret. He poked the lanky youngster until he appeared a bit dazed. The punishment made Ferguson reckless in the sixth and he began to swing powerfully but ineffectively, sometimes missing his mark by a foot or more, while Shirley continued to bore in. Ferguson clinched frequently, to his own disadvantage. He was visibly fagged when the bell sounded. Shirley took Ferguson to the ropes in the seventh and seemed to be nearly to the point of finishing the game when the bell sounded. Both came out with their broadsides in the eighth. Ferguson missed his mark repeatedly and continued to clinch. In this round he succeeded however, in placing his most telling lick, when he sent a right hard directly to Shirley's jaw. The round was Shirley's and when Cal handed the posies there were shouts of approval everywhere.*

***Shirley Wins Verdict in Ferguson Battle,*** *Sterling, Colo. Jan. 26 - Jim Shirley of Denver decisively defeated Mose Ferguson of Julesburg, Colo. in an eight-round bout here Wednesday night. Shirley landed cleaner and more effective punches in every round. Ferguson displayed an unusual amount of gameness. The men are heavyweights.*

An announcement in *The Denver Post* in 1921 read as follows:

***PRELIMINARY***

*Ten round heavyweight boxing bout between*
*Jim Shirley of Denver*
*Runner up in the Denver Athletic Club tournament, 1921*
*and*
*Heinie Zimmerman*
*of St. Francis*
*Denver Athletic Club Champion, 1920*
*All lovers of true sport be sure to see this without fail.*
*POPULAR PRICES $1.50, WAR TAX INCLUDED*

Also, a picture of Jim Shirley on the left and Heinie Zimmerman on the right reads:

***DENVER HEAVYWEIGHT BOXERS WHO MEET WEDNESDAY NIGHT***

*Jim Shirley . . . and Heinie Zimmerman . . . who will go on in the semi-windup at the Stockyards stadium Wednesday evening. Shirley won the amateur championship of the state in 1920 and Zimmerman carried off the fistic honors the year before. They fought a ten-round draw in Kansas two months ago and their encounter here is expected to result in a close battle.*

**Old Celebrities Coming**

Swell dressers, near champions, preliminary boys and the down-and-out stand and chat. A big fellow with a rare design of cauliflower ears, a nose flat against his face and a brow that almost covers his eyes, might be seen talking to some prominent banker. They all mix up for a good time at the Elks' smoker. Many old celebrities will be on hand.

Should Mose Ferguson, the Julesburg heavyweight, win his bout with Jim Shirley of Denver, he will be in line for some important matches in the future. Once the gong sounds after Mose has crawled into the ring, the fireworks start. He never gives his opponent a minute's rest. This has been the history of his battles in the past.

The Fighting Ghost, the dusky boy from the Cole hotel, and Battlink Kid Lucca are in prime condition for their six-round contest.

All of the other boxers in the other four bouts of the program are in the pink of condition and are anxiously waiting for the time to crawl through the ropes.

**Campbell Training Hard**

Ray Campbell and Buster Fitch have employed the best of trainers and messeurs to work them out for their

**Heavies Show Wares**

Mose Ferguson weighed in at 180 pounds, and Jim Shirley of Denver at 175 for the main event. Both proved to be youngsters. Shirley is but 18 years old and Ferguson around 20. Shirley is a well built chap, while Ferguson was angular, with the advantage of several inches in his reach. The Julesburg lad strode about the ring in his robe and grinned at his supporters as they cheered him, for there were many Julesburg fans in the assembly. Shirley sat quietly in his corner. It was announced that they would go eight rounds. Cal. Cheairs was the mediator.

Ferguson opened up by doing a hornpipe about the ring, which added nothing to the confidence that was reposed in him, because there were any number of men present who could dance better than he. Shirley went about his work more cautiously. Ferguson, by reason of his long reach, kept Shirley at arms length during the first round, and while each placed blows there were no signs of a decided advantage for either.

**Experience Proves Value**

The second round also was even; in the third Shirley began to display his better defense and was coming inside the radius of Ferguson's arms. In the clinches he came off to the advantage. In the fourth he further proved his better experience, landing his blows at the spot at which they were aimed. In the fifth Shirley reached Ferguson's nose, to bring the claret. He poked the lanky youngster until he appeared a bit dazed. The punishment made Ferguson reckless [illegible] and he began to swing powerfully but ineffectively, sometimes missing his mark by a foot or more, while Shirley continued to bore in. Ferguson clinched frequently, to his own disadvantage. He was visibly fagged when the bell sounded.

Shirley took Ferguson to the ropes in the seventh and seemed to be nearly to the point of finishing the game when the bell sounded. Both came out with their broadsides in the eighth. Ferguson missed his mark repeatedly and continued to clinch. In this round he succeeded however, in placing his most telling lick, when he sent a hard right directly to Shirley's jaw. The round was Shirley's and when Cal. handed the posies there were shouts of approval everywhere.

## Wednesday Night Bouts at Elks Great Smoke

Mose Ferguson vs. Jim Shirley, eight rounds.

Fighting Ghost vs. Battling Kid Lucca, six rounds.

Stubby Morris vs. Russell Scott, three rounds.

Buck Scott vs. Roscoe Porter, three rounds.

Doc Dorton vs. Fred Whitaker, three rounds.

Ray Campbell vs. Buster Fitch. Have not yet agreed on the number of rounds or anything else. (That's why they're putting on the mitts.)

## Shirley Wins Verdict In Ferguson Battle

Sterling, Colo., Jan. 26.—Jim Shirley of Denver decisively defeated Mose Ferguson of Julesburg, Colo., in an eight-round bout here Wednesday night. Shirley landed cleaner and more effective punches in every round. Ferguson displayed an unusual amount of gameness. The men are heavyweights.

*The Denver Post articles*

Continued:

*SHIRLEY WEARS CROWN NOW FOR LOCAL HEAVIES*

Defeats D.A.C. Champion With Ease - Two Bouts are Knockouts

*by Larry Tate*

*Jim Shirley is now wearing the Denver heavyweight crown. His victory over Heinie Zimmerman, 1920 D.A.C. champion, in the semi-windup of the Wills-Thompson fight Wednesday night gives him a clear claim. Shirley's long left beat Zimmerman every round in their six-round bout. Zimmerman was game but couldn't get started. He made a good comeback in the sixth.*

Another favorite event of Jim's boxing career also came about in 1921. The *Denver Post's* article announced:

*MORE THAN TWENTY OF DENVER'S BEST BOXERS TO APPEAR AT BENEFIT SHOW*

*They are all ready for the gong, more than a score of Denver's patriotic boxers will donate their services at the disabled Yank's smoker to be held at the Aden gym, Thirteenth and Bannock, Friday night. All have been going thru hard training in preparation for the bouts and are in good shape . . . Among the boxers who have volunteered to appear on the benefit program without pay are Jack Doyle, Billy Papke, Big Jim Shirley, Joe Wop Flynn, Al Marker, Jim Miller, Johnny Stopper, Dutch Myers, Drew Daxter, George Manley, Tommy Comiskey, Kid Bell, Dummy Levinsky, Frankie West, Tom Morris, Paul Ahe, Cecil Engel, Kid Hamilton, Tad Hannigan, Young Tendler, Billy Nichols, Don Long, and Harry Gluck. Leonard Lee, Joe Sanders and Heinie Zimmerman also want to display their wares at the smoker. Zimmerman arrived in Denver from the east Sunday and immediately announced that he would be glad to box Big Jim Shirley any number of rounds on Friday's card. The seating capacity of the gym has been increased by circus seats loaned by the Y.M.C.A. Jake Casady will be the announcer and referee the bouts.*

A tournament for the Denver Athletic Club (D.A.C.) was held at the Tramway Club. Harry D. Hoffman, reporting for *The Denver Post* wrote that:

*Jimmy Shirley was the aggressor thruout and kept using a straight left to Charley Miller's face that carried power behind it. In each of the three rounds he scored knockdowns and had his man punch drunk at the finish. Shirley is a two-handed fighter and can shoot a lightening-like right, but withall, it looks as if his left is his big gun for he jarred Miller every time he landed with his portside.*

***DENVER HEAVYWEIGHT HERE***

*Jim Shirley, Denver heavyweight, has arrived in town and wants a crack at any of the local heavies. Shirley has beat Jack Smith, 'Sugar Wee' Keeler, Bob Seroblie, Ed Walsh and many other fast boys. Shirley also holds the Rocky Mountain amateur heavyweight championship, won at Denver in 1921. Shirley is working out at McFarland's gym.*

Some of Jim's contenders became close friends and remained so for many years.

DENVER HEAVYWEIGHT BOXERS WHO MEET WEDNESDAY NIGHT

Jim Shirley, on the left, and Heinie Zimmerman, both of Denver, who will go on in the semi-windup at the Stockyards stadium Wednesday evening. Shirley won the amateur championship of the state in 1920 and Zimmerman carried off the fistic honors the year before. They fought a ten-round draw in Kansas two months ago and their encounter here is expected to result in a close battle.

*The Denver Post 1921*

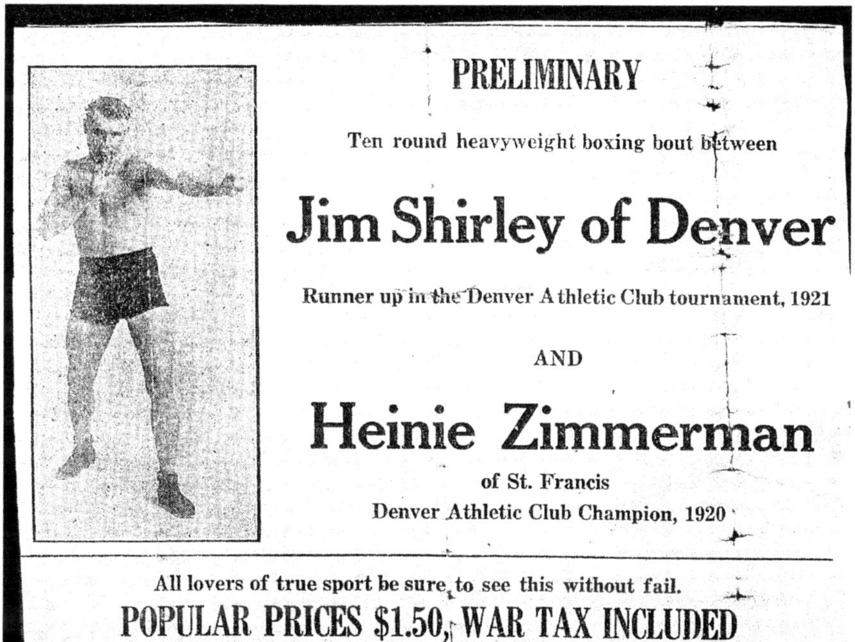

PRELIMINARY

Ten round heavyweight boxing bout between

Jim Shirley of Denver

Runner up in the Denver Athletic Club tournament, 1921

AND

Heinie Zimmerman

of St. Francis

Denver Athletic Club Champion, 1920

All lovers of true sport be sure to see this without fail.

POPULAR PRICES $1.50, WAR TAX INCLUDED

The following is a report by Leslie Showers - Rawlins, Wyoming:

*After angling for a crack at each other for several months, George Manley and Jim Shirley, Denver sockologists, have been matched for a decision bout. They will step twelve rounds in the stellar attraction of a ring card at Rawlins, Wyo. on Labor day. It will be Manley, the clever middleweight, versus Shirley the hard-hitting light-heavyweight. F.W. Morgan, secretary of the Rawlins fire department, who is promoting the show, predicts a record crowd will turn out to witness the soiree. Manley has a large following in Denver who are confident he will dispose of Shirley in handy fashion. Shirley admirers are singing the same song, but to a different tune.*

Jim's career continued in 1921 when Bryant Campbell beat him in the Denver Athletic Club finals. Then Jim had a repeat fight with him and The Denver Post reported:

*Shirley, a vastly improved fighter over his D.A.C. form, knocked the everlasting daylights out of Campbell for two and a half rounds. The referee stopped the fracas in the middle of the third chapter when Jim had Campbell hanging on the ropes punch drunk.*

There was a fight with Charlie Van Cura that Jim remembered well. It went for four rounds to a draw decision. *The Denver Post* reported:

*This was a bout between two fairly clever hard-hitting heavyweights that bristled with action. Van Cura was easy for Shirley's left jab. Shirley was equally easy for Van Cura's hard right counter. It was a fine match. Shirley was out-pointing his man as the bout neared its close. He was also tiring rapidly. A six-round go between the pair should be a gem.*

# SHIRLEY WEARS CROWN NOW FOR LOCAL HEAVIES

## Defeats D. A. C. Champion With Ease—Two Bouts Are Knockouts

By LARRY TATE

Jim Shirley is now wearing the Denver heavyweight crown.

His victory over Heinie Zimmerman, 1920 D. A. C. champion, in the semi-windup of the Wills-Thompson fight Wednesday night gives him a clear claim.

Shirley's long left beat Zimmerman every round in their six-round bout. Zimmerman was game but couldn't get started. He made a good comeback in the sixth.

**Jim Shirley.**

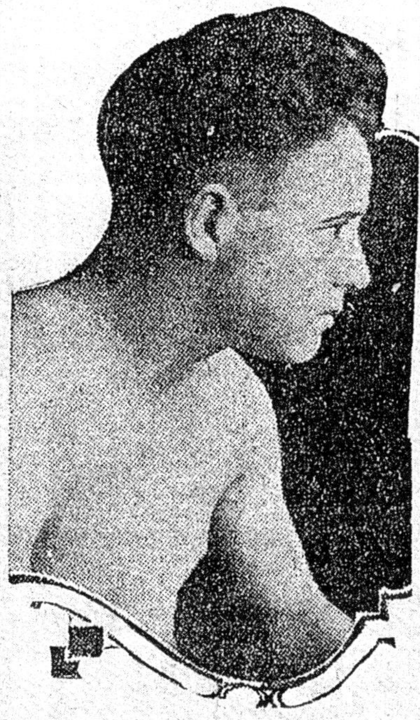

**Local Heavyweight Who May Be Matched With Al Knapp of Colorado Springs.**

*Newspaper articles 1921*

# MORE THAN TWENTY OF DENVER'S BEST BOXERS TO APPEAR AT BENEFIT SHOW

They are all ready for the gong, more than a score of Denver's patriotic boxers, who will donate their services at the disabled Yanks' smoker to be held at the Aden gym, Thirteenth and Bannock, Friday night. All have been going thru hard training in preparation for the bouts and are in good shape.

Numbered among those who will appear is Billy Warner, North Side favorite, who is scheduled to meet Jack O'Brien in a four-round argument. Warner has fully recovered from a recent injury to his right arm and is anxious to again demonstrate that he is just as fast and can hit just as true now as he could before he sustained the injury

Among the boxers who have volunteered to appear on the benefit program, without pay, are Jack Doyle, Billy Papke, Big Jim Shirley, Joe Wop Flynn, Al Marker, Jim Miller, Johnny Stopper, Dutch Myers, Drew Daxter, George Manley, Tommy Comiskey, Kid Bell, Dummy Levinsky, Frankie West, Tom Morris, Paul Abe, Cecil Engel, Kid Hamilton, Tad Hannigan, Young Tendler, Billy Nichols, Don Long, and Harry Gluck.

Leonard Lee, Joe Sanders and Heinie Zimmerman also want to display their wares at the smoker. Zimmerman arrived in Denver from the east Sunday and immediately announced that he would be glad to box Big Jim Shirley any number of rounds on Friday's card.

The seating capacity at the gym has been increased by circus seats loaned by the Y. M. C. A. Jake Casady will be the announcer and referee the bouts.

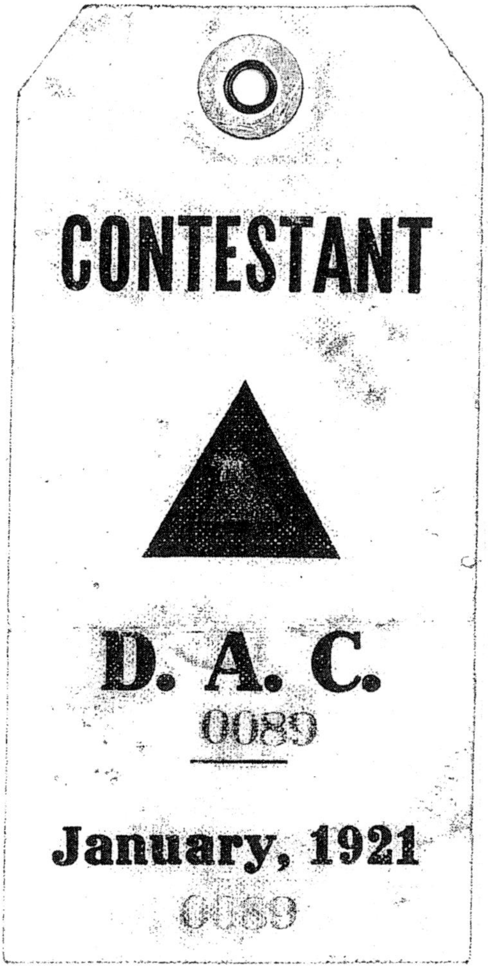
CONTESTANT

D. A. C.

0089

January, 1921

0089

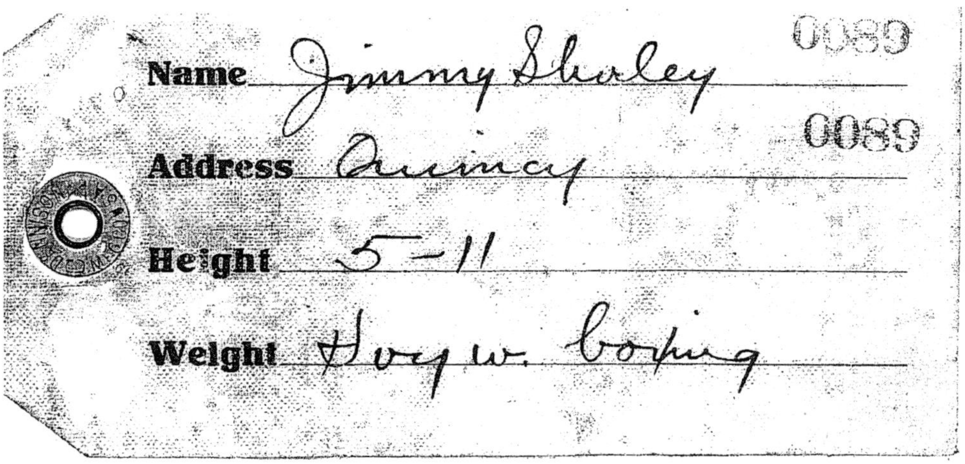
0089

Name Jimmy Shirley

0089

Address Quincy

Height 5-11

Weight Hvy w. boxing

*Jim Shirley D.A.C. tags, 1921*

Unfortunately for Shirley, the story was not good. This was one that he probably did not care to remember for a long time. *The Denver Post* reported:

***Shirley knocked out.*** *Charlie Van Cura came back like lightening from a fierce right-hand hook by Shirley in the second round and the counter swing he landed floored Shirley for as clean and clever a knockout as has been delivered in the stadium for years.*

The fight game was never predictable. It was fought fairly, and the winners and losers went back to their training with hopes of future matches.

The following is one of Jim's engagements that seems quite interesting and must be included for the readers' enjoyment:

*HAYNES WON THE BOOBY PRIZE AT SWAT CARNIVAL*

***Jimmy Shirley, 164 Pounds, Defeated the Kansas Man Mountain, 220 Pounds, and Won Right to Fight for a Gold Watch; Kansaan Gets Razzberry***

*by Harry D. Hoffman*

*Ernest Haynes won the steam-heated ice cream freezer at the D.A.C. carnival of 'give and take' last night. Now Ernest can fold up his tent and return to Colby Kan., and entertain the natives with tales of his prowess and how he won a championship at the big boxing tournament in Denver. The steam-heated ice cream freezer, like the rubberoid nut cracker, is emblematic of the pushing and paw championship of the tournament. There has been heated rivalry for this honor among some of the contestants at the big biff carnival, but Haynes won the honor last night. Pitted against Jimmy Shirley, 164-pound heavyweight from the Quincy gym, Haynes, the 220-pound Man Mountain from Colby Kan., qualified for 'Red' Gallagher's booby prize. For three rounds, Ernest pushed and pushed. Meanwhile Shirley was trying to turn the bout from a pushing match into a fight. He solved the distance between his glove and the Man Mountain's mid section and landed some clean blows. When Ernest wasn't leaning on him and pushing him about the ring he was trying to make a fight out of it. It was a hard job, for the Man Mountain was trying to PUSH him out of the ring. Shirley worked a good left-hand and whatever well-directed, cleanly delivered blows were struck in this embroglio were landed by Shirley. He won the decision over his mammoth opponent, while Ernest was unanimously voted the ice cream freezer with the steam-heater attachment. Haynes' great battle for the booby prize wound up an evening of mitt slinging that pleased the most hyper-critical fan in the audience. By and large it was the best night of the turbulent 10 that has made the1921 tourney a record-breaker.*

There were other boxing encounters during Jim's boxing career in the ring both published and unpublished. The media attention highlighted the previous successes in earning the following titles:

DENVER HEAVYWEIGHT CROWN - in 1920 - age 17
AMATEUR CHAMPIONSHIP OF COLORADO -
in 1921 - age 18
ROCKY MOUNTAIN AMATEUR HEAVYWEIGHT
CHAMPIONSHIP -
in 1921 - age 18 won in Denver

# HAYNES WON THE BOOBY PRIZE AT SWAT CARNIVAL

## Jimmy Shirley, 164 Pounds, Defeated the Kansas Man Mountain, 220 Pounds, and Won Right to Fight for a Gold Watch; Kansaan Gets Razzberry

BY HARRY D. HOFFMAN

Ernest Haynes won the steam-heated ice cream freezer at the D. A. C. carnival of "give and take" last night.

Now Ernest can fold up his tent and return to Colby, Kan., and entertain the natives with tales of his prowess and how he won a championship at the big boxing tournament up in Denver.

Harry D. Hoffman

The steam-heated ice cream freezer, like the rubberoid nut cracker, is emblematic of the pushing and pawing championship of the tournament. There has been heated rivalry for this honor among some of the contestants at the big biff carnival, but Haynes won the honor last night.

Pitted against Jimmy Shirley, 164-pound heavyweight from the Quincy gym, Haynes, the 220-pound Man Mountain from Colby, Kan., qualified for "Red" Gallagher's booby prize.

For three rounds Ernest pushed and pawed. Meanwhile Shirley was trying to turn the bout from a pushing match into a fight. He solved the distance between his glove and the Man Mountain's mid section and landed some clean blows. When Ernest wasn't leaning on him and pushing him about the ring he was trying to make a fight out of it.

It was a hard job, for the Man Mountain was trying to PUSH him out of the ring. Shirley worked a good left-hand and whatever well-directed, cleanly delivered blows were struck in this embroglio were landed by Shirley. He won the decision over his mammoth opponent, while Ernest was unanimously voted the ice cream freezer with the steam-heater attachment.

Haynes' great battle for the booby prize wound up an evening of mitt slinging that pleased the most hypercritical fan in the audience. By and large it was the best night of the turbulent 10 that has made the 1921 tourney a record-breaker.

Bryan Campbell, Tramway club, and Jim Shirley, Quincy club, met for the amateur heavyweight championship.

The go started with both resorting to terrific rushes, when Oh! Campbell's sweet right!—Shirley flopping, all but done for.

Shirley flopped again in the second, but gamely came back in the third until he fell exhausted and knocked out.

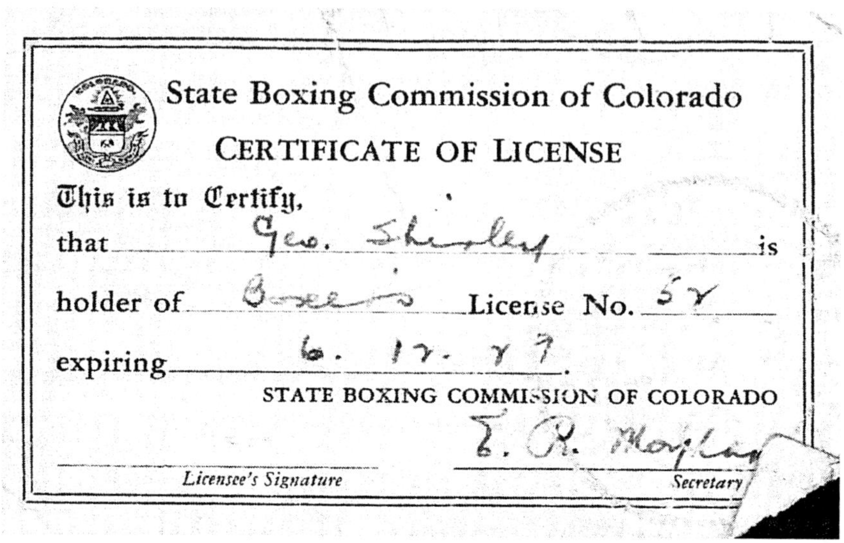

State Boxing Commission of Colorado

CERTIFICATE OF LICENSE

This is to Certify,

that Geo. Shirley is

holder of Boxer's License No. 52

expiring 6. 12. 27.

STATE BOXING COMMISSION OF COLORADO

Licensee's Signature

Secretary

*State Boxing Comission of Colorado Certificate of License for Jim Shirley*

*Denver Post 1921*

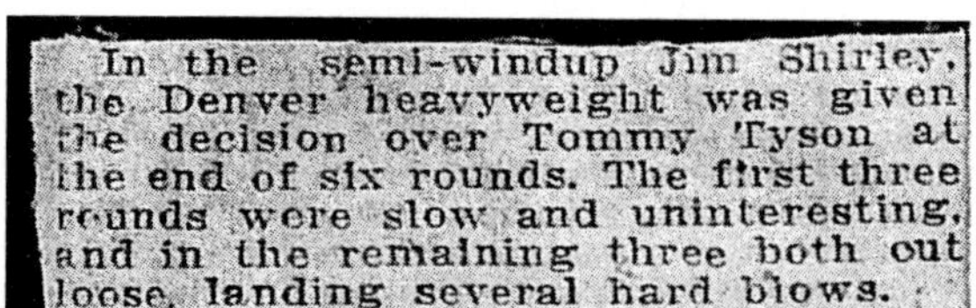

In the semi-windup Jim Shirley, the Denver heavyweight was given the decision over Tommy Tyson at the end of six rounds. The first three rounds were slow and uninteresting, and in the remaining three both cut loose, landing several hard blows.

*Denver Post 1921*

Even though Jim's boxing career occupied much of his time, he enjoyed an active social life when not in the ring.

Young women who worked at the Telephone Company in downtown Denver frequented a local dance hall for relaxation after working hours. This became a magnet for both young men and women to meet each other in a safe and respected atmosphere. Jim was no exception. He looked forward to twirling the girls around the dance floor - and he was popular with the ladies. He met one who especially interested him and they soon became romantically involved. They were both very young. He was eighteen and she a year younger. They knew that their families would not approve of any serious wedding plans at such a young age so, at the height of Jim's boxing career in 1921, they ran off and were married by a Justice of the Peace. A year later, his wife Elizabeth gave birth to a daughter and they named her Margaret. Unfortunately, the marriage did not survive and they were divorced in 1924. Neither could support the baby. Elizabeth's sister and her husband were older and childless. They wanted very much to adopt Margaret and to raise her and give her a good secure home. It was the best solution for all concerned. Jim and Elizabeth remained friends, and Jim made a promise to always remember his daughter and be a part of her life. It was an amicable arrangement.

One of Elizabeth's friends at the Telephone Company also loved to dance. After the divorce, she and her friend Mary would go together to the dances. And that is where Jim met the true love of his life. On the night they met, Mary was standing at the foot of the stairway up to the dance floor while Jim was gazing down at the ladies coming upstairs. Their eyes met and in that instant they both knew they wanted to meet one another. She caught his eye with her flirtatious, sparkling brown eyes. Her auburn-colored hair was set in the latest style with short waves and "spit curls" that framed her pretty round face. She was much shorter than he. Jim found her a joy to be with, and they would dance their hearts out - around and around the dance floor they would go! Mary told Jim of her job at the Telephone Company where she wore head phones and plugged in numbers on a board situated in front of her. She would laugh and explain to him how she would tease and flirt with some of the male callers. Jim, in turn, discussed details of his fighting career.

When Mary shared her intimate story about her family and what a difficult time they had when she was a child, Jim found that he loved her even more for confiding in him. When he asked her to marry him, she knew that this love would last a lifetime.

Both families were a little wary at learning of their engagement since Jim's first marriage had not been successful. Mary was raised a Catholic, and her marriage to a divorced man would not be recognized by the Catholic Church. In spite of all the pitfalls, they ran off to a Justice of the Peace and were married on November 9, 1924. He was twenty-two and she was twenty-one years of age.

Mary chose a beautiful brown velvet dress with a wide lace collar for her wedding. A favorite long pearl necklace hung around her neck. Jim wore a black suit with a white shirt and a striped-colored tie. The wedding picture showed a very attractive and handsome couple.

By this time Jim's boxing career was not his main interest. He began to spend more time at the plastering trade. Mary was instrumental in coaxing Jim to leave his boxing career. She always stated that she didn't want his handsome face destroyed.

Although Jim's family had prospered in Denver, Mary's family struggled to meet the basic economic necessities. She was always conscious of her humble past and was determined that her own new family would never have to struggle as she had.

*James William Shirley and Mary Anne Beran, married November 8, 1924*

*Mary Beran and friend, 1924?*

# CHAPTER III

# MARY'S FAMILY

# MARY'S FAMILY

Mary's mother, Anna Prince, was born in Ord, Nebraska, a small town known for its Bohemian settlement. She and many others had ancestors who had immigrated from Czechoslovakia. At a very young age Anna married Louis Beran. The couple moved to Louisville, Colorado where Louis could practice his trade as a meat cutter. He eventually owned his own butcher shop. The location of the shop was not a good one as it sat alongside the railroad tracks that ran through the edge of town. One day sparks from a train flew onto the roof of the shop and started a fire. Without adequate fire equipment and enough firemen to handle the blaze, the flames spread quickly throughout the building and it burned to the ground. Fortunately it was not occupied at the time. There was no insurance. Since the business was gone, the decision was made to move to Denver.

Anna had already given birth to Mildred and George during that period of time, and was pregnant with her third child.

There was a demand in Denver for experienced meat cutters and Anna's husband was able to find work to support his growing family. They settled in a home at 2708 Bryan Street in Denver. There, on May 2, 1904, Mary Anne was delivered at home by a midwife. This was a common practice in those days. Hospital deliveries were done for only a small percentage of the population.

A fourth child, Louis J. "Bill" was born in 1907. When everything seemed to be going well, a tragedy struck this family. Anna's beloved husband and father of her four children, Louis, passed away suddenly and she was left to raise the children on her own.

After the funeral Anna had to face the sad reality of economic privation as she struggled with her grief. She could not afford to continue to rent the house on Bryant Street, so she hunted until she found a tiny frame house with a chicken coop, a place for a small vegetable garden, and a shelter for the one cow she had purchased with her meager savings. At least, she believed, there would be some food and milk available for her and the children.

Anna did not canvas the neighborhood sufficiently before she moved her family into the house. She soon found that there was a foundry nearby and the noise from it was unbearable with blowing whistles and trucks going and coming at all hours of the day and night. Anna realized that it was impossible to stay in the rented house and that her savings were being depleted by ordinary living expenses.

They would have to move once again. A small farm on the outskirts of town became available for rent. Anna was a very proud and stubborn woman at times. She refused to accept public assistance. To be able to move to the farm, her only sibling, her brother John Prince, came to the rescue. John and his wife Mary lived in Los Angeles, California and were financially able to lend a helping hand. His investments in property in that area had made him a wealthy man. He was a generous and good man. He knew only too well that his sister and the children were in trouble. When the news came that John would send money each month to help, Anna sat down and cried with joy. She expressed her appreciation for John's generosity but let him know that she would only accept enough to cover the bare essentials until she could support her family on her own.

Anna realized how fortunate she was to have such a caring

*Anna Beran's children, left to right: Mildred, George, Bill and Mary*

brother and her thoughts turned to the happy times she and spent with John. With their common Bohemian background, they were both able to speak a West Slavic language. Since it was frowned upon to speak a foreign language in public, people would quietly converse in their native tongue only in the privacy of their home. Foreigners studied the English language so they could pass the required tests to become American citizens. It was a proud event for them and they were happy to conquer the English language. Anna and John were no exception. As proud as they were to speak English, they would still huddle, almost secretly, in a quiet corner and converse in their ancestral language. For some, it was regrettable that their native tongue might not be passed on to future generations. Ever proud of their heritage, families encouraged the use of the mother language in the home. But, once outside the home, English only was the rule.

Anna heard that a wealthy family who lived on top of a nearby hill needed domestic help. The job did not pay well, but Anna needed the job desperately and gladly accepted their offer. Since she could iron beautifully, Anna agreed with the the lady of the house to be paid twenty-five cents an hour to wash and iron her clothes and care for the house. As a holiday gift, the woman would give Anna an extra quarter.

Each day except Sunday, Anna had to walk up and down a steep hill to work. She would return home exhausted. Her small farm required constant attention with feeding the chickens, tending the garden, milking the cow, etc. These chores were divided among the four children. It was a hard life for everyone.

Sunday was a special day. Anna would prepare her Bohemian *kolachies* to the delight of all. She would mix the special non-sweet dough, let it rise for its proper time, roll it out flat and shape it into small squares. Each square was then filled with either a cooked poppy seed or prune mixture. She loved to make them and would demonstrate by putting a spoonful of filling on the center of a dough square and then fold and seal it "diaper-style." The baked delicacy was a culinary delight. She would use this occasion to invite her friends to visit and enjoy the rolls together. After working a full six days with so many hours away from home, this was the treat of the week. However, the children sometimes resented having to share with others. So often they felt there was not enough food for their own family of five. But there always seemed to be enough money for the needed ingredients to make kolachies.

There were no luxuries for this family. There were no "extras." They were indeed very poor. All had limited clothing to wear. Mary told that when she attended school she had only one pair of shoes, a pair of bloomers, a pair of long black socks, a skirt, and a white "middy" blouse. She would have to hand-wash her blouse and bloomers each night, after her many chores, and hope that they would be dry for school the next day. Sometimes she had to stay home from school because she had nothing to wear. The other children had similar problems. But Mary was determined to complete the eighth grade. She knew that education was important. An eighth grade education would prepare her for a decent paying job later. Reading, writing, and arithmetic were priorities, with history being taught seriously with honor and respect. She accomplished her goal, but knew that further education would not be possible for her. Not having adequate clothing and being needed at home to help with endless chores was her unwanted destiny. In large families with limited resources only the oldest child had opportunities to continue their education. In this tradition, Mary's older sister, Mildred, was selected to go to business school.

As the years passed by and the children matured, some good news entered their lives. Anna had been courted for some time by a widower who lived nearby. He had become a constant visitor on Sunday afternoons. The old love bug did its duty! The bride became Mrs. Edward Alfrey. The children approved of their step-father.

Mary found her step-father to be a caring addition to their family. He was a chef, and his artistic abilities flowed when he was in the kitchen working his magic on different kinds of food. Carrots were carved into flowers and fruits of all kinds became individual works of art. When decorating cookies he would transform the icing into funny faces, much to the joy of the children. Mary's favorite concoction was when he transformed mashed potatoes into roses with open petals. And, as time passed, he was the picture of a good husband who treated each of his step-children with love and care.

By this time, Anna's children were young adults. It was a surprise when she told them that she was pregnant. It was not uncommon for women to have babies as they entered their "change of life" in their early forties. The new baby, named after his father Edward, but nicknamed "Little Eddie," entered the world, surrounded by many who wanted to take care of him. Anna worried that he would be hopelessly spoiled, but he showed no ill effects from all the attention. He just cooed and smiled and captured their hearts.

Since Edward was gainfully employed, he and Anna decided it was time to move from the farm to a nice house in the city. They found a brick house to their liking at 61 Elati Street in Denver. It was not large but adequate for the seven of them to be comfortable living in it.

"Little Eddie" was just a few years old when they moved into the new home. Mildred, George, Bill, and Mary were experiencing big changes in their lives. All were employed in occupations in which they were happy.

Mary was dating a handsome young man by the name of Jim Shirley.

Life was good for the family after such difficult times on the farm. But, happiness soon changed to tragedy when "Little Eddie" became desperately ill. They were not sure what caused his sudden death, but sleeping sickness was the doctor's diagnosis. As swiftly as the wind can blow and sweep a little boy up into the heavens, his little life was gone. Needless to say, the entire family was devastated. He had brought so much joy to all of them. They knew the Lord would care for this special little gift.

Even though grief over the loss of "Little Eddie" had engulfed everyone after he had been laid to rest, it was time to move on. New beginnings were inevitable. The marriage of Mary and Jim Shirley offered the perfect opportunity to return to reality and have a celebration. It was natural that Anna, a devout Catholic, was disappointed that the two had run off to a Justice of the Peach for the nuptials but, being a loving mother, she knew that life was not always perfect or within her control. Family love would always be there.

The families joined together for a special dinner to honor Mary and Jim. Mary's step-father, Edward, lovingly prepared the feast. Mary looked down at the tantalizing food placed carefully on the table. It was as if someone had painted a picture of the menu. In the center, on a raised dish, was a large display of Edward's beautiful mashed potatoes all formed into individual white-petal roses. He knew that this creation was one of Mary's favorites. And Mary knew that she would always remember what he had done for her and Jim.

A few months after the wedding celebration, Anna lost her beloved Edward. His illness, like Little Eddie's, lasted only a brief period of time. The family had lost a very dear friend and provider. They grieved his loss to the ultimate. Anna, once again, was a widow with only her children and her memories to comfort her.

Edward's thoughtfulness and financial planning allowed Anna to finally feel secure in her home on Elati Street. Little did she know

*Louis "Bill" Beran, "Little Eddie" Alfrey and George Beran*

*George Beran, Anna Beran Alfrey, and Mary Beran 1924*

that our country was headed for difficult times. In the next few years, changes would be necessary that she could never anticipate.

The Great Depression was just around the corner.

CHAPTER IV

# FLORIDA ODYSSEY

*Mary and Jim in their Model T Ford 1926*

*Mary sitting on the hood of the Model T Ford 1926*

*Mary sitting in front of their tent in "Tent City" St. Petersburg, Florida 1926*

# FLORIDA ODYSSEY

The early 1920s saw an economic boom in Denver, Colorado and the Building Trades had all prospered accordingly. But, in 1925, a cooling off period was very much in evidence. Jim, a plasterer by trade, recognized that if he was to provide adequately for his wife that he would have to look elsewhere for employment. Heeding advice of close friends, he and Mary packed their meager belongings in his small Model T Ford and headed east to a hoped-for land of opportunity.

Arriving in St. Petersburg, Florida after a long and difficult journey, they soon realized that people from all over the country had received the same news of the building boom in St. Petersburg. The availability of housing was nonexistent. Jim and Mary found themselves searching frantically for a place to live. To accommodate the impressive influx of workers, builders and the city fathers quickly assembled a tent city on the outskirts of town. With the ocean as a backdrop, this canvas mecca provided very minimum but adequate shelter for the workers and their families.

Mary discovered all too quickly that bugs, snakes, and flying things were not to her liking as she settled into her humble surroundings. The dry climate of Denver, to which she was accustomed, had not prepared her for the ravages of nature that these winged and crawling beasts could inflict on one's psyche. She especially disliked a large, black, wooly spider that had established residence in one corner of their tent. Her screams brought Jim in a dead run to soothe her frightened feelings. He immediately dispatched the monster to the great beyond.

In spite of her discomfort, Mary found solace in the company of Jim's relatives, Aunt Minnie and Uncle Ed Shirley. They were vacationing from their farm in Atwood, Kansas. Minnie, several years older than Mary, took note of Mary's plight in the land of heat and humidity. Early on Minnie suspected that Mary had more than discomfort to deal with in the excitement of the move to Florida and the drabness of her surroundings. Mary knew that her misery and agitation was more than a passing fancy and, soon afterward, she announced to an excited and jubilant Jim that he was soon to be a father. Minnie and Ed were almost as excited as Jim when the news of Mary's pregnancy was revealed.

In Jim's exuberance over the welcome news, he realized that in their financial crunch he would need to apply himself diligently to the financial well-being of his family. Work was plentiful and lucrative in the plastering trade and he worked long hours, six days a week to capitalize on his opportunities. With a frugal lifestyle and a natural inclination to save his money, the family finances made a dramatic improvement. Soon the young couple decided that the car they were driving would not be big enough for a family. They were elated to be able to trade in the older car toward the purchase of a new one more suitable for their needs. And being able to pay cash for the car made Jim feel triumphant and secure. Also, with the added seating capacity, they were able to share good times and the good life with their many Florida friends.

Mary's discomfort did not detract from leisurely strolls along the beach on late evenings and Sundays with the love of her life - Jim - at her side.

Minnie, though childless, freely shared her feminine knowledge and wise counseling with the young mother-to-be. When the time came for the birth, Mary was so thankful that Minnie and Ed had extended their visit in Florida. On April 9, 1926, Edith Mary Shirley entered the world with a lusty cry, accentuated by the boisterous acclamation of a proud father and a joyous mother. Parenthood put its stamp of approval on this young and loving family. And, it was Minnie who helped care for Mary and the baby when Jim was at work. In the tent city, Mary found comfort in her new friends in like circumstances. She shared her inexperience and misery with her compatriots, and the excitement and business of being a new mother kept Mary reasonably content in her less-than-ideal surroundings.

With farm chores waiting and Mary and little Edith doing quite well on their own, Minnie and Ed decided it was time to return to their home in Atwood. They had enjoyed the trips to the ocean with Mary, Jim, and baby Edith and would miss strolling along the beach in their bathing suits and Edith in her diaper. They would also miss splashing in the cool, salty water. This close family relationship would remain throughout their lives.

The summer heat added to Mary's discomfort as did the sweltering humidity. By September, Mary and Jim were eagerly looking forward to a cooler and dryer fall.

The morning that Mary announced that she was once again expecting created less excitement than they had experienced previously. Though not displeased after such a short interlude, the young couple decided that for Mary's well-being it would be better for the two of them to return to Denver to be near her family.

Jim purchased two train tickets for Mary and baby Edith for their long ride home. Mary made sure that Jim had complete instructions on what to pack in their car when the time came for his return to Denver. There was a tearful and sad farewell at the railroad station, but both knew it was the best thing to do. As the train began to pull out, Mary watched and waved with tearful eyes and a longing heart as an equally tearful Jim faded into the distance.

Without Mary and baby Edith, Jim could not contain his discontent although he knew that he had to make more money before he could rejoin them in Colorado. He intensified his work habits and took all the additional work he could find.

By the end of December, and a lonely Christmas, Jim was more than ready to bid farewell to Florida. It was time to pack the new car. He tried to remember what Mary had told him about their sparse belongings. He did the best he could and headed west for Denver where his beloved wife and baby awaited his return. It was a long, lonely journey home.

Upon arrival in Denver, Jim located the apartment at 1326 Emerson Street that Mary had found for them to live until their home could be built. He was warmly greeted by a very pregnant Mary carrying baby Edith. He couldn't believe how much the baby had grown — so much more than he ever imagined in such a few months. A weary and happy Jim sank into a comfortable over-stuffed chair with his loving family by his side.

After a few days of settling into the small apartment, Jim discussed his vision of a new home with Mary. He started negotiations with a contractor by the name of Dillon to build a house in the outskirts of south Denver. A grade school would be close by and high school was several blocks away. This undeveloped area seemed a good choice. Mary and Jim could not foresee that the growing city of Denver would completely surround this dream home at 1117 South Columbine Street in a few short years.

Jim was grateful for the opportunities presented to him by his employment in Florida. He and Mary had accumulated a sufficient nest-egg to allow them to climb a step-up on the economic ladder

*Mary and baby Edith 1926*

*Jim and baby Edith 1926*

*Mary with two-month-old Edith 1926*

*Mary, baby Edith, Jim, and Minnie and Ed Shirley in St. Petersburg, Florida 1926*

*Mary and baby Edith proudly posing in their new car 1926*

in Denver. They could now dream of owning a home and providing a better life for themselves and a growing family. Jim's working experience in Florida taught him valuable lessons that he carried throughout the remainder of his life. Although he had earned enough for his basic means and beyond, he would never really share in the "Great American Dream" unless he had sufficient clout to bargain with his employer. Without benefits of any kind, he would neither have security nor a voice in his own future. He felt that it was in his best interest to become associated with a labor union with similar goals in mind. The union that most closely met his expectations and skills was the Operative Plasterers and Cement Finishers International Association, Local No. 32 in Denver, his Card No. 56893, and he was initiated (initiation fee paid $75) in July, 1927.

His lifelong love affair with organized labor opened his eyes to a new world of service to others.

CHAPTER V

# PARADISE FOUND

# PARADISE FOUND

Jim, Mary, and baby Edith were still living in the small rented apartment after returning from St. Petersburg, Florida in 1927 when they were notified that their new home in south Denver had been completed. It was ready for occupancy. At the time, the location seemed to be quite a distance from the downtown area but it offered many advantages. There was a shopping area in the 1200 block of South Gaylord and a few blocks away was Washington Park Elementary School. South High School was a short distance from there on Louisiana Avenue. Several blocks to the west was an entrance leading into beautiful Washington Park.

Anyone who has had the opportunity to select and purchase a new home of their very own can appreciate what a thrill it was for Jim and Mary. After finishing touches by the contractor and a close inspection, they were satisfied it was time for the important move.

As they made their way in the Model A Ford heading east on Mississippi Avenue, they crossed University Boulevard. To their left, a large area of mostly vacant lots had been named Bonnie Brae where large expensive homes were being planned for future development. To their right, a few blocks ahead, they made a turn at the corner of South Columbine Street. A vacant lot was on the corner, the second lot had a brick home, and then appeared the pretty pink stucco bungalow with house numbers of 1117 placed at the top of the gabled porch. Bungalows were generally characterized by stone or brick construction, over-hanging eaves, exposed rafters, front porches, and many built-in features. They were typically smaller homes that were built in the late 19th and early 20th centuries.

An inviting porch covered most of the front of the house. As Jim pulled up the concrete-ribbon of driveway, he could see the single unattached garage ahead of him at the end of the house. He had also noticed that the streets were typically covered with gravel and wide cement sidewalks had been poured along the entire block. Each home was separated by a "parking easement." Two trees would be planted there by the city of Denver. The city wanted to be known as "The City of Trees."

Holding baby Edith in her arms, the three ascended the two steps to the front porch. The front and side of the porch were enclosed with a low concrete wall. Mary visualized a wooden flower box that would be placed on top of the low wall and a wooden swing that would be hung from hooks bolted to the ceiling. Since Jim knew about construction he was pleased with the contractor's work.

On one side of the front of the house, French windows circled the south corner. To the right of the front door was a large window. As they entered the front door, they saw French doors folded back separating the living room from the dining room. In cold weather they would be closed to save heat.

Many built-ins included a fireplace with a long wooden mantel. Glassed-in shelves were at the left of the fireplace while wooden enclosed cabinets and a built-in desk were to the right. A very large collection of books would have adequate storage space. Also, toward the ceiling, on each side of the fireplace were two small French windows that could be swung open. A standard window was located to the right and faced the front porch. The walls were all plastered, and some would be covered with wallpaper later as dictated by fashion. The beautifully varnished wooden floors covered most of the rooms except the kitchen areas, bathroom, and rear bedroom.

More built-ins were in the dining room. A large buffet held glass-covered shelves on each side with a mirror in the back. A long linen drawer occupied the lower area. To the left of the room was a large window. A swinging door separated the dining room from the kitchen. There was a window over the sink. On the counter to the right in the corner was a small wooden door called the "cooler." Situated in a more shaded and protected area from the outside, this was to help preserve food. Space was limited with the black cast-iron stove at one side, but a drop-leaf table was placed against the wall and a very tiny table with two matching chairs fit in a corner under the counter for small children.

An opening separated the kitchen from the breakfast nook. A long wooden table and two benches occupied the "nook" space, but because there was no heat to this room, changes were later made. The icebox was still used for preserving food until it was replaced in later years with a refrigerator that took up the space for the table and benches. There was an ironing board that dropped down from an enclosed panel. High French windows that could be pulled open looked over the back yard. To the left of the room was a large enclosed storage cabinet. This cabinet would hold all kinds of useful things over the years.

Two bedrooms were connected to the bathroom with a door leading from each side. A large long closet ran the length of the bathroom with openings on each side. The master bedroom had a standard window, as did the bathroom. The small rear bedroom was used as the nursery. It also had a standard window on the side and French windows that swung open to the back yard. A door separated the nursery from the breakfast nook.

From the breakfast nook area, a flight of stairs with a landing led to the back door. At the bottom, a second flight of stairs led to an unfinished basement. A nice, cool storage cabinet was under the steps. A coal furnace was at the rear of the basement and across from it was an enclosed room for coal. When a new order of coal arrived, a chute was placed in the window of the small room and coal was delivered in that manner. A laundry area with a deep iron tub collected drainage from the washing machine.

After a comfortable pregnancy and a routine move into the new home, the big day arrived! Mary was rushed to St. Anthony's Hospital in Denver where her second daughter, Doris Louise Shirley, was born on June 7, 1927. It had been fourteen months prior that her sister Edith Mary was born on April 9, 1926. Thus began a lifetime of a beautiful relationship between the two girls. Mary always expressed her thanks to the Lord for her two daughters and voiced an opinion that she would never want to bring large numbers of children into the world if she couldn't care for them with a home and enough food to eat. Needless to say, proud Jim again welcomed the new addition with an open heart.

The next few years would be full of many experiences that young families enjoy. Most are wonderful, but sad ones must be accepted also.

Baby Doris was brought home and occupied one of the cribs in the nursery. Edith's crib was next to hers so they always played together.

In addition to the increasing responsibility of a new baby in the house, the young family enjoyed their new home and created their very own way of life. "Projects" were always underway. Two cherry trees were planted in the back yard in the middle of the long strip leading to the alley. A chain-link fence enclosed the entire yard. A strawberry patch occupied the lower end of the yard and hollyhocks thrived beside the pink stucco ash-pit. An alley ran the length of the block so that the garbage collector and ice truck could perform their duties. A card placed in the back window of the house facing the alley designated how large a piece of ice was to be delivered. The iceman would carry the block of ice from his truck and enter the back door yelling "ice man!" The icebox was an important necessity in the summertime. As Jim's work progressed and he was also doing contractor work, the time to replace the icebox with a refrigerator arrived. And what a treat Out went the breakfast table and benches and, as the children grew, the kitchen became too small to eat there. The dining room became the place for all meals.

And there was the chicken coop. It was erected behind the single-car garage. Chicken was at the top of the list for a preferred dinner. It was not uncommon for homes to raise their own fowl, but as Denver grew and became more sophisticated, laws were passed restricting this practice in some neighborhoods. Before this happened, Jim would go out to the chicken coop, make his choice and grab the struggling bird. His hatchet blade was sharp and off came the chicken's head. He would toss it on the ground until it stopped moving. When Grandma Alfrey visited she would grab the bird by the neck, twirl it in the air until it died. Mary would plunge the dead chicken into boiling water that she had prepared on the stove. After a few minutes she would remove it and begin pulling the feathers out. Eyebrow tweezers were used to pluck out the remaining end of the feathers. It was then cleaned and cut up. A large black iron skillet was placed on the hot stove and oil poured into it. The chicken was usually coated with flour, salt, and pepper; sometimes an egg was added to the mixture. That fried chicken was out of this world!

*Adios* to the chicken coop! Flowers occupied the area after the coop was torn down. A swing was set up for the little girls. Summertime was sweet.

Jim owned a shotgun. Since this part of south Denver was still "out in the country," hunting was a favorite sport -- and economically rewarding. South University Boulevard was just beginning to line its streets with new homes. South Colorado Boulevard was considered "really way out in the country." Jim would settle Mary in the front seat of the car and girls rode in the backseat. Driving out to South Colorado Boulevard and taking some side roads, he would pull over and stop. Mary would move to the driver's seat. Jim placed himself solidly on the right front fender. With shotgun held firmly in his right hand, he would wave to her to start driving. Then, suddenly his hand would rise in the air. She would stop instantly. With the gun pointed to the side of the road, there would be a loud blast that would break the silent air on the barren prairie. Jumping from his fender perch, Jim would retrieve his prey -- sometimes a wily jackrabbit. After the return home the rabbit was stripped of its furry covering, cleaned and cut into serving pieces. Mary performed her frying expertise by coating the meat with flour and frying it in the black iron skillet. That mighty shotgun had done its duty again.

After a successful hunting trip, Jim would often stop at the only gas station on the undeveloped South Colorado Boulevard. It was run by a man named Bob who had lost one of his arms. He was a devoted friend of Jim's. With Jim's labeling with outlandish titles to many of his friends and relatives, he always called this special friend, "One-arm Bob." They would laugh and talk to each other with deep affection.

The shotgun also brought down many pheasants on Nebraska farms in later years when Jim was sent for some organizing duties. One summer Mary and the girls joined him and visited friends and enjoyed those delicious pheasant meals that Mary fixed. Jim was never interested in hunting large game.

The numerous trips "going to the mountains" provided delicious trout, caught from cool mountain streams and lakes surrounded by the gorgeous Rocky Mountains. In the kitchen at home Jim would scale them, slit the belly open and remove the innards with his thumb. The fish were washed with cool water and patted dry. Coated with flour, they were placed in the hot oil in that black iron frying pan and fried until crisp on the outside and done on the inside. The tails were usually removed after cleaning. The heads were always removed to make more room in the frying plan. (These procedures were repeated often and will be mentioned again later in our story.)

During one of these fish fry's a near tragedy occurred. The Hestons were visiting — Aunt Mildred, Uncle Jasper, cousins Jack, Junior, and Dorothy. The five children always had a good time playing with each other. The two boys liked being teased by Jim and he would pick them up and sometimes throw them over his shoulder. Usually the sounds of laughter and giggling filled the air. On this occasion, Jim had stopped cleaning fish for a moment and had placed the sharp knife in his back pocket. He did not realize that the blade was upright. Jack returned for some more acrobatic rough-housing. As Jim once again threw him back over his shoulder, he slid down and the knife cut his leg severely. As the blood poured onto the floor, towels were applied to try to stop the bleeding. The cut was not deep and soon everything was under control. A home remedy was applied along with clean rags and Jack survived the order after much screaming and crying. He seemed to always be the victim of unfortunate situations.

During the five-year period on South Columbine Street, the girls attended Washington Park Elementary School. Doris attended Kindergarten and first grade; Edith completed second grade. They walked together the six blocks to school. Mary and Jim had no worry for their safety since neighbors and friends lived all along the way. It was a peaceful and quiet time. Edith began the role of "protector" for her sister Doris. She had assigned the responsibility to herself. She was only fourteen months older, but more serious and mature than her easy-going sister. The name Doris, a male French neighbor insisted to Mary, should be pronounced "Dorrie" with accent on the "ie." Later she was called "Dorie" much of the time. She delighted in making "monkey faces" at her sister Edith to make her laugh. As protector, Edith would give a gentle but serious command whenever there was any prospect of danger. Doris was happy to obey. They were inseparable most of the time, but since they were a year apart in school, they each had some friends of their own.

One cold wintry day, Mary bundled up her little girls in warm coats, hoods, and mittens for their walk to school. The mittens were connected to a string that was inserted though each inside arm of the jackets so they would not lose them. She watched as they went out the back gate, cut across the vacant lot on the other side of the alley, and disappear. She knew they would then go down Mississippi and cross University Boulevard with no problem since few cars used the road. And, of course, Edith was always very watchful.

The weather began a hasty change and temperatures began to drop rapidly. By the time Doris and Edith arrived at school they were shivering. Doris' hands slipped out of her mittens on the way. Tears began rolling down her cheeks. Her little hands were painful. A concerned teacher comforted her and led her to a drinking fountain where she ran cold water over them. Teachers were always there to care in special ways — beyond their call of duty. All ended with no ill effects.

Jim was able to support his family by keeping busy in his plastering trade. He worked on many different types of buildings and there was one in particular that was pertinent to the Shirley family and discussed many times over the years. Movie theaters had become more and more popular after "talkies" arrived in 1927. Beautifully plaster-painted walls and ceilings and ornamented facades were things to behold. One of the grandest of these structures in Denver was the Mayan Theatre on which Jim worked in 1929 and 1930. There was a demand for his decorative and technical plastering skills.

The Mayan Theatre at 110 Broadway in West Denver was formerly the Queen Theatre when it opened in 1916. After being severely damaged by fire in 1938 it had to be completely rebuilt.

During the time that Jim worked on the Mayan, he played a prank on Mary while the indoor scaffolding was still in place. Five Indian head sculptures were being permanently placed on a platform above the stage. She had stopped by for a brief visit to see his work when, by deceit and cunning, he took her by the hand and led her up to the lofty perch, coaxing her to crawl for a close-up look at the faces of the Indian heads. He retreated and left her stranded high above the floor. Only her pleas of mercy brought him to her rescue. She always said that she made sure the he never pulled a prank like that again!

On the lobby walls of the Mayan, a brief history of the name of the theater was posted. It told about the height of the Mayan civilization, the only literate society in pre-Columbian America where kings believed in the power of the pen. Scribes played a central role in magnifying their king's reputation and solidifying his political hold on the realm. During the Classic Mayan period, 600 to 900 A.D., the scribes were held in high esteem because of their paintings and sculptures. Court scribes came from the noble class and sometimes the royal family itself. In this Classic period there were at least forty city-states across the heart of the Mayan domain which included what is now southern Mexico, Guatemala, Belize, and Honduras. The civilization went into sharp decline around 900 A.D.

*Mayan Head Sculptures above stage of the Mayan Theatre*

*The Mayan Theatre at 110 Broadway in Denver, Colorado*

*Below: Details of sculptures in the Mayan Theatre*

An issue of *The Denver Post*, dated June 18, 1984, reported some facts about the Mayan Theatre as follows:

*"...the evening of Nov. 20, 1930, when the Indians camped out all night and chanted on the roof of the Mayan Theater. The Indians' antics caused quite a stir and some annoyance in the neighborhood. The night was the beginning of the 'Mayan spell.'*
*The drum-beating tribe of American Indians carried flaming torches through the building to exorcise evil spirits out of the theater before its grand opening in 1930.*

*The theater was operated by the Fox Intermountain chain, and the main feature that evening was 'Monte Carlo' starring Jeanette MacDonald and Jack Buchanan."*

Aztec and Mayan polychrome trim and a terra-cotta Indian Chief adorns the front of the Mayan Theatre. Terra-cotta, translated from the Italian "baked earth," is a hard, semi-fired waterproof ceramic clay used in pottery and building construction. It is grayish to dark reddish orange, light or reddish brown or deep orange in color. The clay was mined locally from a ridge between Boulder and Golden. It was popular between 1910 and 1930 and the Mayan Theatre was one of the last to have had this building material used.

Since Edith and I were quite young during the time from 1927 to 1933 when we lived in our brand new South Columbine Street residence, only a few recollections of events that took place at that time can be written about accurately. Some of the stories relayed are those that were repeated during gatherings of family and friends. The following is one that may be of interest to the reader.

Mary and Jim always loved going to both horse and dog races. Horse racing was not as popular during this time, but dog racing had become a welcome diversion. Somehow they acquired some greyhounds to be entered for racing at the local race track. The unfinished basement of the house was selected as the kennel. One of the dogs was named "Digie" and was the favorite because of her sweet disposition.

The story told was that the dogs were very susceptible to health problems resulting in diarrhea. Also, they would become "erratic" at times and jump up on the concrete walls to reach the windows and chew on the wooden frames. Of course, there was always the necessity to clean-up after them. Since Jim had to be at work many hours of the day, caring for the dogs was left to Mary. Besides taking care of Edith and Doris, she also kept busy preparing a special "stew" for the dogs since their stomachs could not tolerate many other foods. Needless to say, Mary became quite irritated as the chief caregiver and head chef for the greyhounds. She and Jim quickly discovered that greyhounds were a high-maintenance operation and not a money-making venture.

One day there was bad news. Digie had disappeared. They searched all over the neighborhood and far beyond, but Digie was not to be found.

It was obvious that the time had come to give up the greyhounds. Mary was more than a little relieved when the last dog found a new home. She vowed never to undertake animal husbandry as an occupation.

Months later, when the family was driving in north Denver to visit some friends, Jim suddenly stopped the car. He said that he had spotted Digie down the street. Sure enough, they all agreed that it was Digie, happily playing with some children. Jim didn't have the heart to go claim her when he saw how well she looked. There was no encouragement from Mary to rescue Digie as they drove by without stopping. Thus ended the great greyhound story!

A picture of Edith and me on the back yard swing set as youngsters and another picture of us in front of the house sitting in a wagon led by a billy goat with a sign "1929" on it are beyond my memory. Also, as babies, Edith and I were photographed sitting on top of a cement banister while visiting grandparents at their South Pearl Street home (shadow in the background was someone holding on to us).

A picture of our half-sister Margaret, Edith, and me taken March 27, 1930, was very memorable. Jim is shown posing with his three daughters as we were bringing a gift to Margaret. I am holding it in my hands. He always made sure that we had visits throughout the year with Margaret on her birthday, holidays, and a full day visit in the summer when we weren't in school. Edith and I would be taken to her home and always enjoyed a fun time with her.

There are faint memories of celebrations. One was at Christmastime when Jim always brought the biggest, live evergreen tree he could find that would fit in the living room. He enjoyed this tradition and continued it for many years no matter where we lived.

As noted previously, the coal furnace provided adequate heat for the house, but the French doors leading from the dining room into the living room were kept closed during very cold days to save on coal. Jim would wear a warm sweater as he decorated the beloved Christmas tree. He added beautiful ornaments each year to his collection. He would hang each one tenderly on the lush green branches. After stringing the lights, he placed long green and red ropes on the branches around the entire tree. Silver icicles were then hung, one by one, over the entire tree, gleaming brightly as the light him them. The final decoration was a shiny silver star placed carefully at the very top of the tree.

On Christmas morning, Edith and I would run as fast as we could to that cold living room to see what Santa Claus had left for us under the tree. There was great excitement and anticipation as we joyfully gathered our precious gifts. Little did we know that this celebration would undergo some dramatic changes when our financial circumstances required that we move to West Irvington Place.

*Doris and Edith Shirley as toddlers on backyard swing*

*Doris and Edith Shirley with goat and cart*

*James Shirley with Margaret Johnston, Edith and Doris March 27, 1930*

The New York Stock Exchange reported that the Dow drifted downward after the peak of 381.17 on September 1, 1929. Although the date of October 29, 1929, Black Tuesday was probably best known by the public, many historians say the crash began Thursday, October 24 and accelerated the following Monday and Tuesday. From its close at 305.85 on October 23, the Dow tumbled 75.78, or 24.8% by the time it ended at 230.07 on Black Tuesday. Stocks kept falling as the Great Depression wore on, and the Dow fell to 41.22 on July 8, 1932 giving it a loss of 339.95 from the September 1929 high.

Prices collapsed amid panic selling and thousands of investors were wiped out as the Great Depression in America worsened.

By 1932, one in four Coloradoans was unemployed. Only one in eight made more than $5,000 annually (in 1936 one in seven).

In Denver, there continued to be enough construction work for qualified men who could build the needed structures, so Jim was gainfully employed in his trade as a plasterer from 1927 until October of 1929. He was always grateful and proud that he had been initiated in the Operative Plasterers and Cement Finishers International Association of the United States and Canada, Member No. 56893, Local No. 32 in Denver, Colorado in July, 1927.

Jim became more and more active in his union and he and Mary's closest friendships were formed with those who had a common bond through the union. The friends were constant visitors in our home, usually playing cards and enjoying each others' company. Our family, in turn, visited in their homes also.

The Great Depression continued to show its ugly head. Most all vocations were feeling the loss of jobs. The construction trades were being hit hard.

When building ceases, it means that there is no work.

No work means no income.

What this all meant was that families such as ours had their very livelihood affected to the point that changes had to be made to survive.

Each day Jim and Mary were feeling the pressure. His only plastering jobs were becoming scarcer and scarcer. Their financial condition was becoming very critical.

They made the important decision that they had to move to save their home. There was a $2,000 loan remaining on the house. If payments were not made immediately they would lose their home.

Fortunately, Mary's Uncle John Prince who lived in California was a wealthy man due to real estate investments. As soon as he heard of their predicament, he offered to send them the $2,000 without any interest and no timetable to repay it. In that way, they could move to a much less expensive place and rent out their house. The rent would more than pay for a small, suitable apartment, and they would be able to save something to repay Uncle John. They agreed that they would open a savings account and vowed to put at least something in it, no matter how small, whenever possible. Uncle John reassured them that there would be no hurry for them to repay the money. They were grateful for the great generosity of this very unselfish man.

Both Mary and Jim were familiar with a particular neighborhood on the west side of town. Mary had lived at 61 Elati Street before she married Jim and knew of a grade school only a few blocks away with a nice park nearby. Jim knew of it when he worked on the Mayan Theatre which was not far from South Broadway.

There was a small, four-unit apartment house on the corner of Elati Street and West Irvington Place and a vacancy was available on the second floor of one of the units. The landlord showed them the apartment which was very small and lacked frills that they were used to in their home, but the rent was very reasonable. And they knew that they would have to get used to the absence of gas for heating and cooking.

The family moved from 1117 South Columbine Street to 365 West Irvington Place in June of 1933.

They did not know of the tough times ahead.

Their "Paradise Found" would be "Paradise Lost" for awhile but strength and perseverance and the help of the Lord will get them through it!

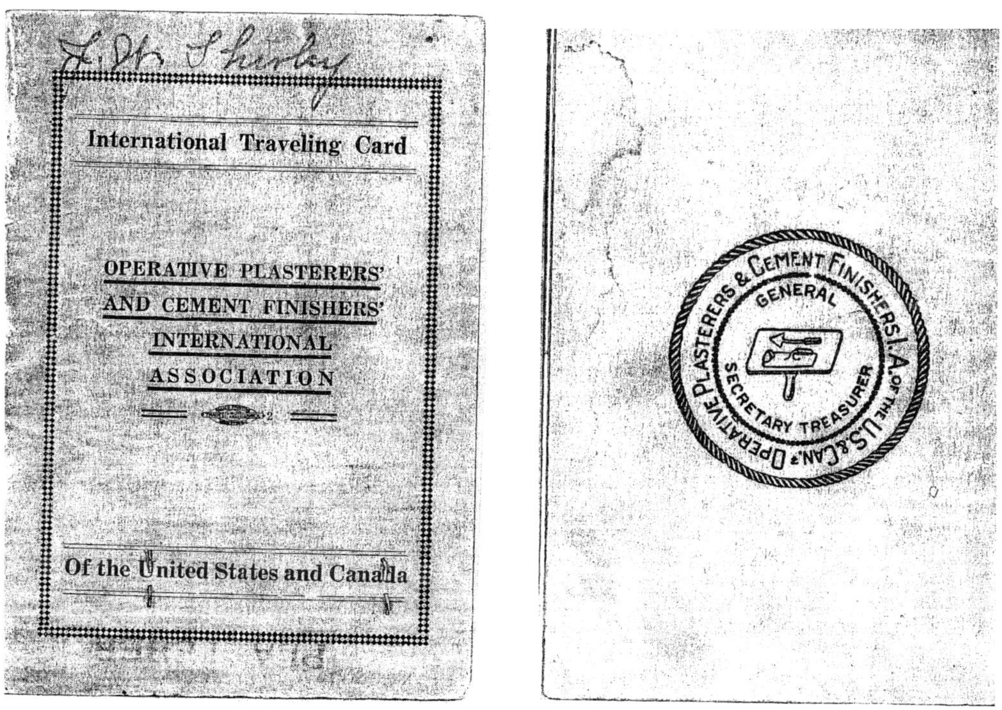


*International Traveling Card*

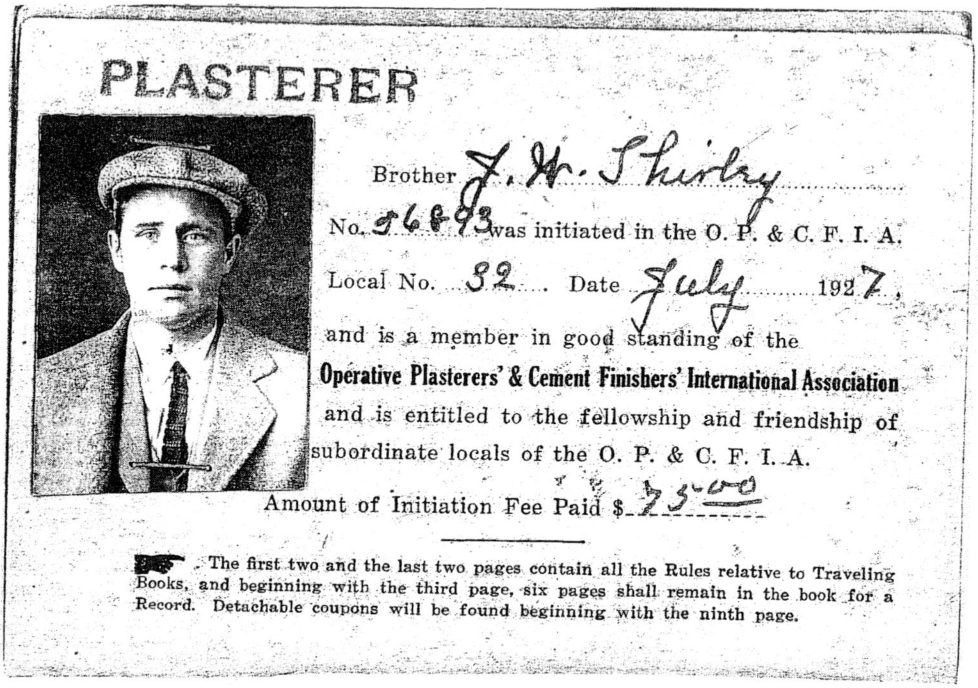

PLASTERER

Brother J. W. Shirley

No. 56893 was initiated in the O. P. & C. F. I. A.

Local No. 32 Date July 1927

and is a member in good standing of the

**Operative Plasterers' & Cement Finishers' International Association**

and is entitled to the fellowship and friendship of subordinate locals of the O. P. & C. F. I. A.

Amount of Initiation Fee Paid $ 75.00

The first two and the last two pages contain all the Rules relative to Traveling Books, and beginning with the third page, six pages shall remain in the book for a Record. Detachable coupons will be found beginning with the ninth page.

*Plasterer membership cards*

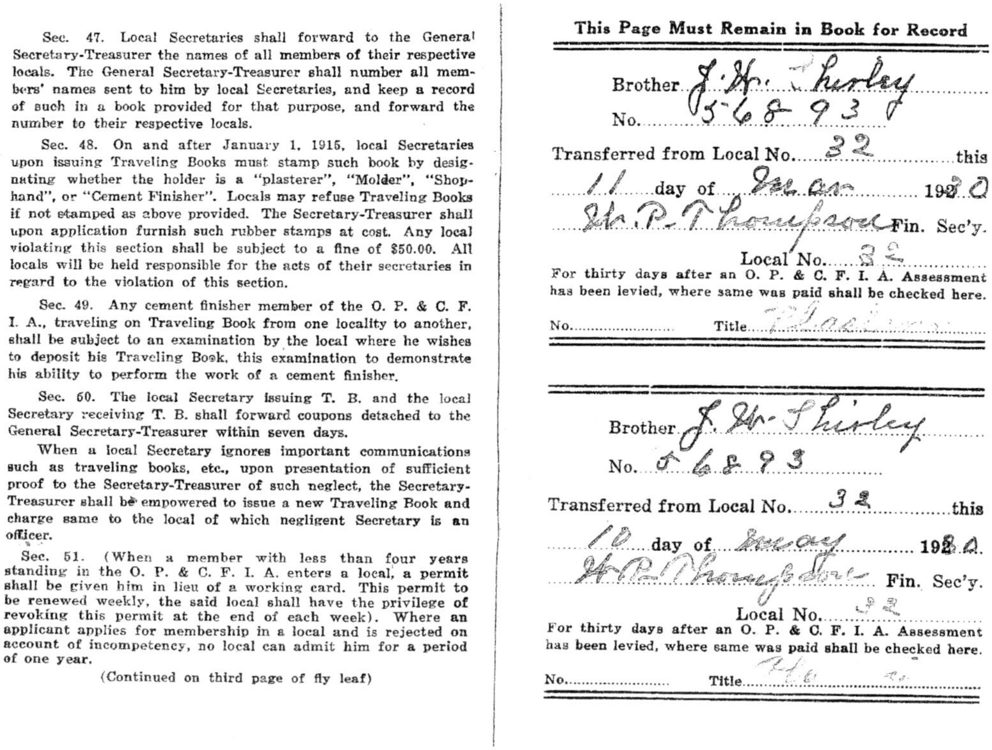

Sec. 47. Local Secretaries shall forward to the General Secretary-Treasurer the names of all members of their respective locals. The General Secretary-Treasurer shall number all members' names sent to him by local Secretaries, and keep a record of such in a book provided for that purpose, and forward the number to their respective locals.

Sec. 48. On and after January 1, 1915, local Secretaries upon issuing Traveling Books must stamp such book by designating whether the holder is a "plasterer", "Molder", "Shop-hand", or "Cement Finisher". Locals may refuse Traveling Books if not stamped as above provided. The Secretary-Treasurer shall upon application furnish such rubber stamps at cost. Any local violating this section shall be subject to a fine of $50.00. All locals will be held responsible for the acts of their secretaries in regard to the violation of this section.

Sec. 49. Any cement finisher member of the O. P. & C. F. I. A., traveling on Traveling Book from one locality to another, shall be subject to an examination by the local where he wishes to deposit his Traveling Book, this examination to demonstrate his ability to perform the work of a cement finisher.

Sec. 50. The local Secretary issuing T. B. and the local Secretary receiving T. B. shall forward coupons detached to the General Secretary-Treasurer within seven days.

When a local Secretary ignores important communications such as traveling books, etc., upon presentation of sufficient proof to the Secretary-Treasurer of such neglect, the Secretary-Treasurer shall be empowered to issue a new Traveling Book and charge same to the local of which negligent Secretary is an officer.

Sec. 51. (When a member with less than four years standing in the O. P. & C. F. I. A. enters a local, a permit shall be given him in lieu of a working card. This permit to be renewed weekly, the said local shall have the privilege of revoking this permit at the end of each week). Where an applicant applies for membership in a local and is rejected on account of incompetency, no local can admit him for a period of one year.

(Continued on third page of fly leaf)

**This Page Must Remain in Book for Record**

Brother J. W. Shirley
No. 56893
Transferred from Local No. 32 this
11 day of Mar 1920
W. P. Thompson Fin. Sec'y.
Local No. 32
For thirty days after an O. P. & C. F. I. A. Assessment has been levied, where same was paid shall be checked here.
No. Title Plasterer

Brother J. W. Shirley
No. 56893
Transferred from Local No. 32 this
10 day of May 1920
W. P. Thompson Fin. Sec'y.
Local No. 32
For thirty days after an O. P. & C. F. I. A. Assessment has been levied, where same was paid shall be checked here.
No. Title Plasterer

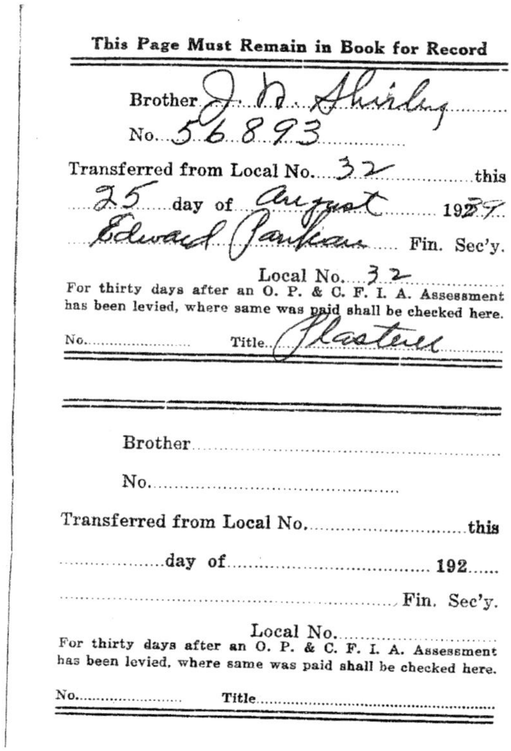

**This Page Must Remain in Book for Record**

Brother J. W. Shirley
No. 56893
Transferred from Local No. 32 this
25 day of August 1927
Edward Parker Fin. Sec'y.
Local No. 32
For thirty days after an O. P. & C. F. I. A. Assessment has been levied, where same was paid shall be checked here.
No. Title Plasterer

Brother
No.
Transferred from Local No. this
day of 192
Fin. Sec'y.
Local No.
For thirty days after an O. P. & C. F. I. A. Assessment has been levied, where same was paid shall be checked here.
No. Title

*Pages from Book of Record for J.W. Shirley*

*Mary and John Prince, June 24, 1913*

# SURVIVING ON THE EDGE

Edith and I had just finished our school year at Washington Park Elementary School in June of 1933. I was six years old and Edith seven when our family moved to our new residence at 365 West Irvington Place in west Denver. A lot of my memories at that particular time are very vivid in my mind; others, as can be expected, remain like hazy shadows in the dusty corners of some room. At times, stories were repeated at family gatherings when I was present and I believe them to be accurate as I recall them.

It seemed as though the move from 1117 South Columbine Street in south Denver had been uneventful. Our new home was in a pleasant-appearing neighborhood with a mixture of dwellings. Our particular block was lined with both masonry and frame homes and with this one small apartment house in which we would live. A row of terraces were located in the rear, facing Elati Street. Our four-unit apartment house had two lower and two upstairs apartments, separated by a common wall.

Daddy opened the front door and led us up the wooden staircase to the second floor. At the head of the stairs, straight ahead, was a bathroom that was to be shared with the downstairs tenants. As we looked in we saw a white porcelain washstand, toilet, and a deep, large-footed bathtub. To our right was a landing stacked high with cardboard boxes holding unpacked miscellaneous household items. Next to them was the door that led into the apartment. Mother began unpacking some of the boxes while Daddy was instructing the movers where to put the large pieces of furniture. Edith and I did our best to stay out of their way.

*Top photo: 365 West Irvington Place taken in early 2000's*

*Middle photo: Entrance to the upper and lower apartments at 365 West Irvington Place*

*Bottom right: The author standing in front of 365 West Irvington Place*

By evening the move was completed. As I stepped into the living room I saw only one small window that faced east. Dim light filtered through sheer curtains that were hung in front of a rolled-up window shade. A tall lamp stood in a corner of the room providing light, but its dark shade did not produce adequate brightness. The room seemed a little eerie to me as dark shadows danced about on the walls like ghosts and focused on an assortment of framed pictures. Mother had already hung a favorite above the sofa. It showed an Indian sitting on his pony. Dressed for battle, he pointed a spear skyward in a defiant gesture. I remembered it well from our other home. A small magazine table had been placed between two overstuffed chairs. A wool rug covered the center of the wooden floor. A bookcase in the corner held our treasured collection of books.

The only bedroom in the three-room apartment was in the front and faced the street. A full-sized bed had been squeezed into the small space of an alcove in the bedroom and that was where Edith and I would sleep. A full bedroom set filled the remaining space and was where Mother and Daddy's sleeping accommodations were.

The kitchen was located in the rear. Mother had already cooked our supper on the portable Coleman stove since the weather was warm. The Coleman will be replaced by the large cast iron stove sitting on one side of the room when the weather turns cold. Since space was limited, the dining room furniture had been sold before the move. A wooden table with four chairs, an ice box, a radio on a stand, and a washing machine filled the kitchen space. A large pantry was at one end of the room.

Mother was always neat as a pin. A full apron was usually worn over her cotton house dress as she worked diligently around the kitchen to prepare the meals for her family. A large spoon in her right hand stirred whatever she was cooking. The air was filled with the aroma of something good to eat.

The disadvantage of the second floor apartment was the location of the exit from the kitchen. It opened to a small outside landing with wooden stairs leading to the ground below. Beneath and a few feet to the right were the storage bins for wood and coal. To the left was the small parking lot and also the clotheslines. A walk along the back of the row of terraces led to the alley where the garbage cans sat on top of an ash pit. There was no grass. There were no flowers.

Mother served the tasty home-made soup and passed a bowl of soda crackers. Daddy always ate more than one bowl of soup. Milk was poured for all, followed by pie, cake, pudding, or Jell-O — whatever she had available. We always had food to eat. We never left the table with an empty stomach.

But the seriousness of the situation regarding the Building and Construction Trades Industry was continuing to be hit hard. Many building projects had virtually come to a standstill. It was affecting all tradesmen drastically. Daddy was very aware of the happenings. His only plastering jobs now were very small ones called "patch" jobs. They did not pay well. Grandpa Shirley - "Pa" as Daddy called him - notified him of any jobs he heard about, but the requests had become almost nil. It was time to seek other type of work!

Even before the move, Daddy informed Mother that he had heard about a company named *Watkins* that was hiring people to sell their products door-to-door. After discussing the possibilities of a different kind of job with her, he immediately called the company requesting an application for one of their positions. They made arrangements to see him. He drove to their office and after a lengthy interview, he was hired! When he returned home with the great news there was celebration with lots of hugs and kisses in the Shirley household.

Daddy discussed with Mother the many changes regarding what he was going to need, including some new clothes. He had been advised that a white shirt and proper trousers had to be worn each day on his route. Mother was the shopper. She knew that they could not be second-hand items, so she shopped diligently in the downtown department stores for just the proper attire.

The Watkins Company furnished Daddy with a sample kit and a small order pad. In the palm of his hand he would be able to write an order after he placed a piece of carbon paper between the two forms. The original would be given to the customer and the second copy he kept as his record of the sale. He examined the sample products one by one. Included in the inventory were many cooking items such as spices, pie fillings, extracts, flavorings, pudding mixes, etc., plus household and personal grooming products. They were also pictured in a separate catalogue. The retail price for an item was numbered for his information and to place an order with the company. He and Mother were excited about the new job and very thankful that they had a car for him to cover a large route.

The first day on the new job arrived. A new white shirt showed beneath a jacket and the trousers were clean and neat. As Mother gave him a good-bye kiss and wished him much luck, one can imagine what must have passed through her mind. With his Irish good looks and dashing personality, she probably knew that he would impress his customers, especially the females.

Now a whole different lifestyle began. Mother still had as many household chores as before and shopping for the best buys in grocery stores remained the same. But she began using many of the Watkins products herself. The company discount prices for employees were very helpful. As she tried the powdered pie fillings and other food items, she was quite surprised to find that some were very delicious. She was known for her pie crusts — an art that her beloved late step-father had taught her. When she baked one of her pies with a Watkins filling, it was a treat. The company was well-known for its pure vanilla extract. She approved of it also. Our family began using many of the personal items such as the shampoo. Also, a favorite was a menthol ointment that came in a round green metal can, nicknamed "green salve" by our family. Every time someone got a cold, our parents would smear our neck and chest with it and push an added glob up into our nostrils. A clean old dish towel was then wrapped around our neck and secured with a large safety pin. As time went on, that salve was used for many afflictions.

Each evening when Daddy returned home from his new job, he was full of smiles. He would sit down on a chair in the kitchen and tell us all about his customers and selling Watkins products door-to-door. He related to us how he demonstrated the shampoo by taking a tiny portion and placing it on the back of his hand — his hairy hand. Rubbing it gently and then wiping it off, it showed the remarkably clean results. He told about some really nice lady customers who treated him with respect. They probably knew that he was trying to feed his family and to survive the Great

Depression. When they were ready to order he produced his order book. He showed us how he would wet his finger with is tongue so he could flip through each page easily. He was careful to check the addresses and names and what was ordered. To finally place the orders with the company, he called them on the telephone from home. Later he drove to the warehouse and picked up each order. He found it was not a very substantial income but it was helping the budget to survive. He hoped that in time sales would increase.

Even with the change in lifestyle, Daddy never changed his intense interest in the labor movement. His evenings were still filled with important union meetings. Loyal friends to their cause remained the same. Hard times did not change the numerous social get-togethers with relatives and friends.

Edith and I adapted easily to the new surroundings. We still talked about the "flower dolls" that we used to create from the backyard of our previous home. We would collect four-o'clock flowers and sometimes hollyhocks and pinch off their "heads." Then we would layer them into a full petal skirt, thus making the "doll." It was a profitable enterprise as we would appear at one of our neighbor's doors and try to sell them for a penny a piece. By kindness alone, a purchase was made for five of them. That made our day! But new experiences will begin in our young lives, different ones that we will never forget.

It was the highlight of the day for Mother, Edith, and me when Daddy arrived home from work and we would all be standing in the small living room. It was evident that there was always a strong loving attachment between my parents. They laughed a lot and they kissed a lot. As I mentioned before, Daddy was a big man. His height of just under six feet was quite a contrast to

Mother's five-feet two inches. His blue eyes identified the Irish blood that flowed through his veins. And his dark, curly hair, which he hated and tried to keep held down with oil, framed a handsome face. A muscular body showed evidence of the earlier boxing career, and his nickname from that former era, "Big Jim Shirley," fitted him well. As Mother stood in the room, Daddy's concentration was on her. His Mary was indeed the love of his life. Her dark auburn-colored hair shone as the light from the ceiling danced and reflected upon it. She was a very pretty and petite woman. Her face was all smiles when her Jim entered the room. He held her in his arms and stared into her dark brown eyes that always had a special glint of mischievousness in them. With a wide smile she would grin at him as they hugged and shared a long-awaited kiss.

One evening when Daddy returned home from his sales job with Watkins, he brought great news. The Annual Picnic of Denver Watkins Dealers was to take place on July 23, 1933. He had only been working for them about a month and a half so it was a pleasant surprise that he was invited also. And best of all, all family members were included, even extended relatives. Edith and I were elated! A picnic of any kind was a rare and special treat. Daddy sat down with Mother and they made a list of people they thought they should invite. Daddy's sister Claire and her husband Paul from Fort Collins were first on the list. Hopefully they would be able to leave their florist shop for the long outing. Others to be invited were Grandpa Shirley (Pa) and Grandma Martha, Grandma Alfrey (Anna) and the Hestons (Mildred, Jasper, Dorothy, Jack, and Junior).

Positive replies for the July 23 Watkins Picnic from all of those invited were good news. Everyone would be able to attend. They were informed that a special panoramic picture was to be taken just before the picnic started. Our guests appeared as instructed and the picture was taken.

The weather had turned into a beautiful summer day and the bright sun spread itself over the picnic area like streaks of silver reflecting from a nearby lake. The park's green grass was a welcome sight. We children removed our shoes and ran through the cool, prickly, velvet covering. A large temporary tent had been set up to cover tables and benches and to keep the food protected. All of the food, beverages, and prizes for the many competitions were furnished by the company. My very favorite activity was getting all the ice cream I could eat. And no wonder this was such a special time for Mother. She didn't have to prepare and pack all of the food as she did for our many trips to the mountains and other outings.

After our sumptuous feast, the races began. Everyone who wanted to enter was welcome to do so. The first was the gunnysack race. One had to hobble to the finish line holding up their sack with both legs inside. There were many who did not make it as they tumbled to the ground in a fit of laughter. The next was a three-legged race whereby one person's right leg was tied to another's left leg. This was also disaster for most contenders.

Next came a favorite and considered the best of all — the shoe-kicking contest. Mother and Aunt Mildred had been practicing for weeks to see how far each could kick their shoe. Of course, the person whose shoe was kicked the farthest was the winner. When this event was announced, all of the ladies lined up and began taking their turn. Aunt Mildred kicked hers first — it almost landed on her head! Moans and whistles erupted from the numerous on-lookers. Then it was Mother's turn. She slowly got her shoe positioned just right on the tip of her toe and, lo and behold, it floated through the air like a bird taking flight. The judges marked her distance on the ground. She was the winner! Watkins products, consisting of an assortment of choices, were awarded to the winners. Mother chose a box of her favorite pie mix.

Toward the end of the day as the sun was gradually disappearing behind the majestic Rocky Mountains to the west, a pale, sobbing little girl was running toward the family car. Just before she got there, the vomiting began. It was me. I had eaten an unlimited amount of ice cream, so much more than I should have (famous last words). It came as a surprise to Mother since she knew I was not a "urpy" child. But she knew my love for sweets, so she was not too shocked. She always remembered that she had to hide dessert from me at suppertime, usually in the pantry, or I would not eat the proper food that she had prepared for the family.

As Mother cleaned me up, I'm sure she gave special thanks to the Lord that I had finished getting sick before I reached the car. If I had gotten inside and continued to be sick, it would have been an unpleasant and very smelly ride home—to say the least!

The Watkins picnic was a highlight of that summer and since all of the children were out of school during the months of June, July, and August it was the time for families to get together. Our family was no exception.

Daddy's Watkins job was helping financially but not substantially. He had accumulated more customers, but the fabric of the economic situation in our country made it difficult for people to make ends meet. They did not have adequate resources to generate more income. And his plastering patch jobs were very rare.

The blessing was that the Denver weather was warm and outside social activities prospered because of it.

The year of 1933 would not be complete without including the visits of family members. It was always one of those very special times when Mother's sister, Mildred, would bring her three children — Dorothy, Jack, and Junior — to see us. An announcement that the Hestons were coming brought great joy to Edith and me as these cousins were close to us. Junior, named after his father, Jasper Emerald, was the youngest and we considered him the baby. Jack was the middle child and his age was just between Edith's and mine. Dorothy was the oldest and four years older than Jack. In child years that was quite a difference and she always seemed to be quieter, more dignified, and more knowledgeable. In her superior roll, she could be quite bossy, but the other four of us didn't pay much attention and went ahead with our own fun plans.

I remember a warm summer day when the Hestons arrived for a visit. Daddy had just assembled his Watkins kit, placed his order book in his pocket, and had the car keys in his hand. His bright white shirt was tucked carefully into the waist of his freshly-pressed trousers, and his well-polished black shoes gave off a subtle glint. His usual big hug and kiss from Edith and me was the normal routine. Mother smiled as he held her in his arms and then he gave her a kiss that lingered for awhile.

The front door opened and four Hestons arrived. Grandma Alfrey, who at times also came, had stayed home. Uncle Jasper was at work and sometimes joined us later. Daddy grabbed each of the boys and gave them an enjoyable rough and tough time. Dorothy had a much milder reception and was hugged tenderly.

And now it was Aunt Mildred's turn and she knew she would be teased in some way. (Edith and I always addressed our adult relatives with their proper title). Aunt Mildred was energetic, fun-loving, and known for being good-hearted. As the saying goes, she would "give you the shirt off her back" whenever help was needed. As Daddy made his way to the back door he waived a farewell and added, "Have a good time with that 'sack of nuts'" as he grinned at his sister-in-law. With his kidding remark, she laughed profusely and waved him out the door. Mother followed him to the back porch to make sure he hadn't forgotten anything. They were such a young and devoted couple, dealing with all of

*Annual Picnic Denver Watkins Dealers - First Section*

*Annual Picnic Denver Watkins Dealers - Second Section*

the hardships and uncertainties at this difficult time.

(As the author, it has always been difficult for me to realize how young my parents were. In the summer of 1933, Jim Shirley was 31 and Mary was 29. As I recall these wonderful get-togethers, I can see them in my mind as being much older. It is strange how our childhood memories remain with us fixed in time.)

As Mother returned to the kitchen, non-stop chattering began between her and Mildred. There was much to bring up-to-date. Daddy always said that the two of them never paid much attention to the other and what they were saying. But somehow, by some sisterly miracle, they seemed to understand the subject being discussed. Deciding the agenda for the day required considerable compromise.

Four of us cousins began playing a game while Dorothy put

her nose in a book. Since Junior was the baby, he was sometimes picked on by us, but he could hold his own very well in a rather stubborn, serious manner. He had a slight lisp that made some words and sentences sound cute. We all adored him when he would recite something like, "abie yes, abie 'ot." He also was a healthy child unlike his brother Jack. Poor Jack seemed to be the one that had unpleasant things happen to him. He had always been a sickly child. Aunt Mildred told of having to raise him on goat's milk because of his tender digestive system. But he was the jovial one who laughed a lot and was always so good-natured.

The big event of the day was a trip to the nearby potato chip factory. It was located about a block or so down the street from the mom and pop store on the corner. The factory sold their potato chip seconds to hungry walk-in customers. They were always fresh, delicious — and cheap! A small 6-ounce bag sold for one cent. The four of us cousins were given a nickel each. We strolled down the few blocks to the building. As we entered a large room there was a man standing in front of a long counter. We made our way toward him in single file, each holding our precious nickel. The first one in line asked for five bags of potato chips. The clerk grabbed a metal scoop and began filling a small paper sack to almost over-flowing with the flavorful product. The odor of cooking oil filled the air. We each waited patiently for our turn. When the last order was filled, we carefully carried our fragile goodies in our small arms. Only when we returned home were we allowed to savor our first chip. One was allowed to indulge while Mother made sure that generous portions were saved for the rest of the family.

As lunchtime approached, Mother decided to send Dorothy

and me to the corner grocery store. It was a very small store but it carried many everyday essentials — and a large candy counter. I was instructed to help Dorothy carry the packages home. As we entered the store, a male grocery clerk awaited our order. Dorothy ordered a dime's worth of bologna which would be an ample amount for sandwiches for all of us. There was a large slicing machine on a table near the door. The clerk placed a very large roll of bologna next to the sharp blades and sliced the required amount. As he was slicing the meat I couldn't help noticing that he had a small dark growth on his upper lip. It was like a dark-colored mole. As he sliced, his head seemed to keep in time, but the mole never moved. (I'm really not sure why I was fascinated with that mole; perhaps childish interest.) He then pulled a piece of brown butcher paper from a large roll, cut it off, and wrapped the meat tightly. Dorothy then asked for two quarts of milk at eight cents each, and a large loaf of white sliced bread for nine cents. There was always an unwritten law with the family that whoever went to the store got to keep the penny or two in change to pay for some candy. Dorothy and I each chose a favorite penny candy from that wonderful glass-enclosed candy counter. We devoured the welcome treat as we made our way home.

In the afternoon, Mother took Mildred out the front door to see the stump of a tree that was located near the apartment house. To their delight a huge mass of mushrooms had grown all over the top and sides of the stump. Their first impulse was to pick them, then cook and eat them. But they were worried as to whether they were poisonous or not. Mother explained that she had heard that if you boiled them in water with a silver dime and the dime did not turn black they would be alright to eat. If the dime changed to black, that meant that you should not eat them. They both agreed there was a possibility that the story was not true. Neither wanted to take a chance and become ill, or worse. Temptation gnawed at their very being. Mushrooms were too expensive to buy with their meager food budgets. Suddenly, almost out of nowhere, a small Oriental woman came walking up the sidewalk. She was holding a large paper sack. She asked them if it was alright for her to take some of the mushrooms. Aunt Mildred glanced at Mother with a surprised and shocked look. After a brief consultation, they made a heart-wrenching decision to let her have all the mushrooms she wanted. Happily, after filling her bag and picking most of them, she bowed repeatedly and skipped merrily away out of sight. They never knew what happened to her — or to the mushrooms, poisonous or not.

It was now mid-afternoon and swimming time. All of the Hestons had brought their bathing suits and were changing into them. Edith and I were already dressed in ours. The sun provided nice weather for our short walk to "Sunken Gardens" near West High School. The small shallow pool was warm and a welcome relief from playing games at home. Other children were also enjoying the pool. Aunt Mildred and Mother found a nice cozy place to sit on the green grass and watch the children having a good time. After awhile some older boys appeared and seemed intent on disrupting the smaller children in the pool. Usually our mother and Aunt Mildred would take a bold stance to end this type of situation. The bullying and threatening continued and the mothers knew they were out-numbered. It was time to head for home.

As evening was settling in, it was time for Daddy and Uncle Jasper to return home from their jobs. Uncle Jasper was a very likeable and lovable man. He had survived his tour of duty in France during World War I, after which he had met and married our Aunt Mildred. Since she was the talker, he would sit silently and gaze at you with his kind blue eyes. He, indeed, had earned the title of a good and loyal husband and father.

After a dinner of fried hamburgers, potatoes, and vegetables, all prepared on the portable Coleman stove, Mother served a pudding that she had prepared from one of the Watkins products. She also opened a quart jar of her home canned fruit that was kept on one of the shelves in the pantry.

As the family joined together on the front steps and sidewalk much later in the evening, it was time for that ultimate treat — ice cream! Since the icebox was limited in keeping items cold or frozen - and price was a factor - ice cream was always reserved for special occasions. A trip to the corner grocery store produced a box of twelve ice cream bars. Each bar was molded on a flat wooden stick. There were always two bars marked *FREE* in the sealed box, but the *FREE* label on the wooden stick was hidden beneath the vanilla ice cream and chocolate covering. What a wonderful discovery when a *FREE* bar was found! The winner would dash back to the store and turn it in for another bar at no cost.

Unfortunately, in later years, that winning treat had to be discontinued. Crooks found a way to mark the sticks themselves with dark printing and would locate a merchant with poor eyesight, present the imitation stick, and receive the award. Only an uncaring and undisciplined person could perform such an ugly and despicable act.

Another Heston family visit presented a challenge for Mother and Aunt Mildred. They had seen pictures in ads of celebrities sporting their *crowning glories* in a beautiful deep red hair color. Henna was supposed to be the secret. So, on one particular visit, they both decided that they wanted to try this risky procedure on their locks. They could use one bottle between them. Aunt Mildred's hair was more on the brownish side while Mother's had natural red (auburn) highlights. They took a walk up to South Broadway where a drugstore was located and made their purchase. They knew their husbands would not approve since real ladies did not dye their hair. But they were undaunted in their quest to beautify themselves. They returned home with their questionable purchase.

With wet heads covered with bath towels, Mother and Aunt Mildred awaited the instructed time for the henna to do its job. As they each carefully lifted the bath towels from their heads to see the promised result, it was a shock of disaster! They had dreamed of only a light touch-up, but both heads of hair had turned a very deep red — no — almost a very deep orange-red! They began rinsing the color out over and over again. Each took turns washing then rinsing in the pan in the sink. After several times, some of the color seemed to fade. Now it was time for their husbands to return home from work. The ladies met them at the door with their heads covered. Fortunately, men don't seem to notice things as much as women and no comments were made. When they finally removed their head coverings, nobody said anything! That ended the henna look forever.

The day after Labor Day in September was when Edith and I went to school at Fairmont Elementary School. The school was only a few blocks away and was built in 1924 in the Collegiate Gothic style by architect Harry James Manning. While the exterior featured arched entrances, special care had been taken with interior decoration depicting birds and animals for the children to enjoy. This is where Edith and I attended school beginning in 1933. She was seven years old and in the third grade and I was six years old and in the second grade. We both had entered kindergarten at the age of four when we had lived in South Denver. This was an acceptable choice in the Denver Public School system at that time if the child was academically able to pass certain tests and other qualifications. We both did well in school; however, Edith seemed to be the better student. Since she was a year ahead of me with a report card of all ones (A's), her teachers would welcome me with the same expectations as she had represented. Being a little slower, it made me work harder to keep up that reputation and my marks of two (B) seemed to work better for my ability. I think I could have been a very happy 3 (C). She was always an honor-roll student. I usually missed that mark by a few points in the grading system.

Fairmont Elementary School offered a diverse number of classroom opportunities. One was an Auditorium Class that each child was obligated to attend. Since it was in the auditorium, there was a stage. The teacher would send an assignment home to the parents when it was their child's turn to memorize a poem to recite to their classmates. I remember well when it was my turn to prepare for this event. I ran home from school and excitedly told Mother and Daddy that the next day I was to memorize and recite a poem all by myself on the stage. With a wry twist to his mouth and a bright twinkle in his mischievous eyes, Daddy said that he would teach me something to recite. It was: "There was a little Dutchman who drank a lot of beer, and his big tummy stuck way out here!" Then he told me to point to my tummy with both hands in a grand gesture, and then bow.

The following day the auditorium teacher called my name. I ascended the steps, walked to the center of the stage and proudly, with a loud voice, recited the memorized poem that Daddy had taught me. The other children laughed loudly to my delight. The teacher, however, with a surprised look and a frown on her face, gave the knot of braided hair on the back of her head a quick jerky movement. She reach down and picked up a book lying on the floor at the side of the stage, opened it to a desired page, and handed it to me. She instructed me to read the poem. It was a simple one and I did as I was told. Later at home, I told my parents that the teacher's poem wasn't nearly as good as Daddy's.

Since Edith was in the Auditorium Class a year ahead of me, they were more advanced and were actually taught to take part in stage productions. It was now her turn to be excited as she informed Mother and Daddy that her class was to perform the play, *Snow White and the Seven Dwarfs*. It was to be produced for the entire school to attend. This was quite an undertaking. Edith announced that she had been selected to play the part of Snow White. With great pride, Daddy's "buttons burst from his shirt" as the old saying goes. Mother also joined in with praise. They both knew that she was capable of handling the part as she was a very special daughter. And she indeed fitted the part well. Her pretty round face with unblemished, smooth very fair skin, black hair, brown eyes, and a nicely formed nose was a picture of Snow White. She had a quiet and sweet disposition. They also knew

*Fairmont Elementary School with Author in front*

that she could memorize the part easily as she was an exceptional student. Learning came easy for her and she excelled in everything she did.

Preparation for the play was lengthy, but the big day finally arrived and Daddy took off work so he could attend and sit beside

Mother in the auditorium. I sat in the balcony with my classmates and watched as the children shuffled about on the large stage below. We could see that some needed a little coaxing from the sidelines. This was quite a challenge for those so young. They did a good job and deserved the loud applause from the audience and the praise from teachers, parents, and friends.

That evening at home, Mother fixed a special supper to celebrate Edith's success. I recalled a scene when Edith as Snow White was surrounded by the Seven Dwarfs. I couldn't believe how pretty my sister looked.

A class that Edith and I both enjoyed attending was *Library*. This room was known for its wonderful collection of books donated by a retired school board member in 1925. The walls were covered with shelves and bookcases that held all kinds of books and related materials. All around the room just below the ceiling level were paintings depicting the search for the Holy Grail. We were so impressed with this story that we would routinely relate to our parents about how our library teacher, Miss Lort, would tell a segment of the continued search as a special treat each week.

Miss Lort would also introduce us to pictures of other countries around the world through a device called a *stereoscope*. This was an optical instrument held in our hands through which two slightly different views of a scene were presented, one to each eye, giving a three-dimensional effect. We children would take turns looking at those fascinating and interesting pictures. She would explain other cultures to us in great detail.

We enjoyed our library teacher's ability to speak rapidly in catchy phrases, such as "Peter Piper picked a peck of pickled peppers," repeating it several times as fast as possible. We would try to imitate the phrase as she did and found it difficult - but fun!

Gym class presented some challenges for me. Edith did not seem to have the problems I had with certain physical exercises. I could never climb the rope. My arms did not want to cooperate in that difficult task. But one game I enjoyed was when the entire class, both boys and girls, ran relay races. I was a good runner. On one relay day, we were lined up in rows with about six children in a line. The gym teacher said to run as fast as we could to the metal lockers that lined the end of the gym, touch the locker, and then run back as fast as we could and be sure to tag the next participant in your line. The line that finished first with all of its runners in would be the winner.

My turn came. I was tagged. I took off as fast as my legs would carry me toward those metal lockers. I slammed my right hand as hard as I could at the locker and pain immediately caused me much distress. I held my right arm and ran as fast as I could, but a little slower this time as the pain was getting worse. I managed to tag the next team member but the pain was so severe by this time that I fell down on the wooden floor. The gym teacher immediately took me to the school nurse's office. They called home and within minutes my Mother was there to hold a crying and hurting girl. Somehow she got me home and very shortly thereafter Daddy came home. They took me to a doctor who was located on South Broadway. This was a different experience because when Edith and I had been ill, our parents took care of us themselves through all kinds of childhood cuts, bruises, diseases, etc. They worried this time that I had broken my arm. Thankfully it was just a sprain. This meant that I could not use the arm for awhile and had to wear a support to protect it. This made me a hit at school as I was the only one wearing a white sling to hold my arm. I became the envy of the class. Another plus was that I could not take my turn at washing dishes. Edith and I had a routine of helping Mother with the dirty dishes. This was supposed to help earn our allowance for that popular Saturday movie. We usually took turns on who had to wash the dishes and who had to dry them. Of course, this was all by hand using cotton dishcloths and towels. I was indeed lucky. I couldn't handle either of the chores, but I did put the dishes away in the pantry. Wow! How easy could it get?

Another routine on Monday mornings, Mother would lay two white handkerchiefs on the kitchen table. She would carefully place a nickel and a dime on each one. Then she would roll and tie the money in the handkerchief. Next she would take a safety pin and secure it to each of our dresses. This was our milk money. When we arrived at school our teacher removed the money from its pouch. Then at mid-morning, those who took milk were sent to the lunchroom. A small bottle of milk, a graham cracker, and a small paper napkin were provided. I personally loved the routine. And even though the cost was small, there were always some children's parents who could not pay the three cents a day for milk. At times, I saw the teacher reach into her own pocket and pay for a child who could not afford it. I was thin and thoroughly enjoyed taking milk, but Edith tired of it and refused the milk routine. Mother didn't insist as her weight seemed adequate and she was a very healthy girl.

When the weather was quite chilly, Mother insisted that we girls wear long stockings to school. Since the stockings were held up with a garter belt with elastic holders, they were both uncomfortable and looked awful. I hated wearing them. Edith reported (or snitched) to Mother that I would roll mine down below the knee just before I reached the school grounds. I called Edith a tattletale and a fight began. To settle the dispute Mother went shopping and returned home with some new long stockings for each of us. She explained that the new ones were not heavy like the old ones and were part rayon to appear more silky. She showed us the label to prove her point. I was convinced and knew that my mother would never lie to me.

With the new stockings held up with those pinch garters, Edith and I left from the back, walked behind the row of terraces to the alley, then on to the corner where the little mom and pop store was located. We crossed the street and made our way two blocks farther to school. And then, just before we got to the playground, I released those garters on my new stockings, rolled them down to just below my knees, and danced happily on my way.

Edith just shrugged her shoulders.

There was always a beehive of excitement going on in our household. Card games, such as pinochle and poker, were popular with Mother and Daddy. They would get together with friends on Saturday nights, visiting and enjoying each other's company and sometimes in different homes.

Ballroom dancing was also a favorite of all as they would meet at a crowded dance hall, laughing and having a great time. Edith and I were always included. We would play in the cloak room, running and hiding among the maze of coats that hung above us. Sometimes Daddy would come and get us for a turn around the dance floor by bracing us one at a time on top of his shoes, or just holding our hands to swing us in time with the music. Mother loved to dance and she and Daddy seemed to enjoy themselves immensely. After all, their first dates were at a dance hall before they were married. Edith and I would return to a cozy place in the cloak room where Mr. Sandman soon put us to sleep.

In spite of Daddy's long working hours and spending time with his family, he always attended the Union Hall meetings which took place on some evenings. He was very proud to carry his Operative Plasterers and Cement Finishers union card.

It had been a good summer and fall in spite of the constant worry of money to meet expenses. Daddy knew too well that his Watkins income would drop off soon with winter approaching. Little did he know how bad it was going to be.

Winter arrived. By early evening snowflakes were beginning to float gently through the crisp air as if to keep in time with a beautiful song. The weather had changed abruptly which was not unusual for Denver. Temperatures could fluctuate rapidly in a twenty-four hour period. The sun seemed to be the one dependable gift of nature as it would shine in all its glory most days of the year in this part of the country. The majestic Rocky Mountains to the west of the Mile High City seemed to cover the horizon forever. As I would gaze in their direction they looked like sleeping giants joined together with their jagged and imposing peaks covered with blankets of glistening white snow.

I can still remember the sound of my father's car as it turned the corner on Elati Street and pulled into the parking lot. Snow had begun to cover the dirt surface. A multi-clothesline, supported at each end with study posts, occupied a small part of the area. After Daddy parked the car he walked around the corner to our front door. Edith and I always waited and listened for Daddy's return home as Mother kept the supper warm on the iron stove. Sometimes we leaned over the wooden banister to see him climb upwards to our second floor apartment and other times we waited inside and watched for the doorknob to turn so we could surprise him as he entered the room. After working on a plastering job his heavy work shoes were usually covered with dollops of dry white plaster. There was a noisy thud on each step as he wearily made his way up the wooden staircase. He worked a very long twelve-hour day but always let it be known that he was grateful for the work. Even though he always looked tired, he would reach down and gather us up into his strong arms for a welcome hug and kiss. Mother was always there to add more needed love and affection.

The early winter had begun with freezing temperatures and more snow was in the forecast. This meant more trips up and down the back staircase, mostly for Mother, as she was home all the hours that Daddy had to work. More wood and coal was needed, garbage had to be taken to the alley, and snow and ice had to be kept off of the outside stairs.

Edith and I were always bundled up from head to toe so we could walk to school and back home again.

Daddy had found a small plastering job for a female doctor. Unfortunately, some of the work was on the outside of her home where the snow had covered the ground and the temperature had dropped drastically. But, again, he was thankful for the job. Daddy was a very proud man. He made it clear over and over again that he didn't want to go on relief. For most, they did not have a choice.

One evening Mother had prepared supper for Daddy's return from work as she always did, but this night she sensed something was wrong. Edith and I had begun to worry also. She tried to comfort us as she always wanted to protect us from unhappy circumstances. This time became different. It was the sound of Daddy's footsteps as he was making his way up the stairs in the hallway. There were slow and hesitating - not his usual bouncy sound. Also, there was an unfamiliar sound that came through the door. Mother was really worried now as a frown creased her forehead. The sound she heard was that of loud uncontrolled coughing. As Daddy stumbled into the room, Mother helped him into the kitchen and settled him in a chair next to the warm stove. He told her that he had been working high up on a scaffold at the doctor's house when he began coughing severely. But he kept on plastering. Then he became light-headed. The kind doctor gave him some cough syrup. But when the coughing got worse and blood appeared in his sputum, she told him that he must go home. She also told him that it appeared that he had a case of whooping cough and that it was necessary for him to get some rest. There were no paid benefits for the working man at that time; there was no health insurance; there were no paid vacations; there was no workers' compensation of any kind for such emergencies. Daddy said that he had expressed his thanks to the doctor for her help. But he was terribly worried. He knew that he did not get any pay at all when he could not work. He repeated over and over again to Mother that they needed money to live on. His Watkins job was not doing well. She did her best to console him and to assure him that everything would be all right.

Edith and I cried as Mother put us to bed. We did not like seeing our daddy so ill. There was also the concern that the rest of us could catch this terrible disease.

The coughing got worse. One night after Edith and I were asleep, Mother was with Daddy in the kitchen when all of a sudden she said Daddy leaned hard over the empty coal bucket in a spasm of coughing and fainted head-first into it. She rushed to his aid and started pulling him upward with all of her limited strength. He indeed was a big man. Much to her dismay, his head stuck steadfast inside the coal bucket. Then, suddenly, he regained consciousness much to the relief of Mother. With both of them helping, they gently pulled the bucket off of his head. But by doing so, the sharp insides of the bucket cut nasty wounds on either side of his forehead. She tended to the cuts with her home remedies.

Soon he began recovering as the coughing stopped. The wounds were healing well. That special chicken soup Mother fed him must have been responsible for some of the healing. They were thankful that no one else caught the whooping cough.

The story was told for many years. Not everybody gets a coal bucket stuck on their head! And now we continue after the *Winter from Hell*.

••••••••••••••••••••••••••••••••

Good news arrived after the whooping cough experience. Mother was informed by the landlord that the downstairs apartment was to be vacated soon. It would cost a few dollars a month more for rent but had more advantages than the current upstairs location. The arrangement of the rooms was better. There was a living room at the front that faced the street and a fireplace at the outside wall. A large dining room opened from there. At the end there was a very small bedroom in the rear near the kitchen. There would be privacy as the dining room could become Mother and Daddy's bedroom. It could hold the full bedroom set of a bed, dresser, and chest of drawers. Edith and I could use the bedroom in the rear. Since it was very small, it would hold only the double bed and a small dresser, but would be very adequate for us. Even though the kitchen was smaller, the washing machine could be stored on the back porch. Also, Mother could carry her wash around the building to the vacant lot where the clotheslines were situated and make it easier for her. The storage bins and garbage cans were located much better also. The bathroom was not in a good location since it was shared with the upstairs occupants. Everything could not be perfect. After all was discussed, the move took place.

One of the first things Mother did was to make a trip to a rummage sale. She found curtains for the new apartment at a very reasonable price. She always had a knack for fixing up windows and other decorating projects. Household items and clothing were also on her list at those sales when she had enough money to purchase them, and that was always a problem. She would wash the items first as soon as she returned home and then soaked them in Rit dye to produce a color she desired. Then she starched them before the final ironing. The objects would look great when she was through. When people came to look at the vacant upstairs apartment and then saw ours, they frequently commented that if the upstairs looked as good as the downstairs, they might be interested in it. She seemed flattered but her main hope was that we would have good neighbors.

The new kitchen on the ground level was the center of most of our many activities. Fuel was difficult to come by and keeping a supply of coal and wood for the kitchen stove was a chore itself. Even though the fireplace in the living room was available, it was seldom used. The sleeping accommodations for Mother and Daddy with their bedroom set in the dining room worked out well. And Edith and I enjoyed our little bedroom.

Bathing was the same as before with Mother, Edith, and I sharing the wash tub in the kitchen. Mother still heated water on the coal stove, but now she had to carry it up the stairs to the only bathroom for Daddy when he returned from a very tiring work day. Since weekly bathing was limited, spit baths were done on a regular basis in a small pan that was set in the kitchen sink. It was amazing how a good scrubbing was accomplished in that limited space.

Trips to the Denver Public Bathhouse were fun for swimming and a substitute for a good bath. One of those trips to the bathhouse that was memorable to me was when the Hestons — Aunt Mildred, cousins Jack and Junior — came for a visit so that we would all go to the bathhouse. We all walked up West Irvington Place to South Broadway where we rode a streetcar to the bathhouse. After entering a large door, we formed a line and each of us was handed a bar of soap and a towel. Lockers were provided for our clothing as we changed into our swimming suits. Adults were required to wear swim hats also. It was requested that everybody shower and then step into a pan of disinfectant before entering the pool. I hated that pan of smelly water and tried to walk around it, but I didn't get away with it. An attendant pointed to it and I knew that they meant to enforce the rule for everyone. Males and females were supposed to be separated, but Aunt Mildred tried to sneak Jack in with her. She shoved a large shower cap over his head, almost covering his eyes, and his pair of trunks didn't do a good job of covering his private parts. But that was Aunt Mildred! She insisted that he stay with her. Needless to say, she got away with her deception as she led him into the pool under her protection as Junior waded in the small kiddies' pool. We all really enjoyed swimming and then gratefully took those wonderful showers afterward before we made our way back home.

The people who occupied the row of terraces just behind the apartment house were all very poor. Some had only a single person and others had large families crowded into small rooms. There was one quite elderly lady who welcomed a visit from us children. One day, Edith and I knocked on her door and she invited us in for a cup of tea — her specialty. The place was dark and musty-smelling. She had a clothesline strung across the kitchen where tea bags were hung by clothespins. They all looked like they had been used many times. She poured each of us a cup of hot water, released one of the tea bags from its clothespin, and dipped it once in each cup. This was a treat from a very sweet, lonely, kind lady. We thanked her as we had been taught to do and skipped merrily home.

Two events that were popular to draw people from their terrace homes were the *rag-sheeny* man and the *ice man*. The former would buy anything for a small price — even gunny sacks (burlap bags) — and would announce his coming down the alley by yelling, "Rags! Bottles!" The second event was the ice man. It was a treat for all of us children. We would run to the back of the truck and wait for him to shave off some delicious slivers of ice. We would grab a piece and suck on it. His job was to clamp giant ice tongs around a large chunk of ice and go to the back screen door and announce in a shouting voice, "Ice man!" Without hesitation, he would enter and place the block of ice in the icebox in the kitchen whether anyone was home or not. He would know what size to deliver by the *ice card* that hung in the window. It indicated the number of pounds ordered.

Most of our neighbors did not have a car so this was an excellent service. Since Daddy owned a car he would stop at an ice house on his way home from work, choose an appropriate block of ice, place it in a burlap bag, and tie it to the front bumper. When he arrived home he would remove the burlap bag, clamp tongs around the block of ice, and place it in the icebox in the kitchen. It was cheaper for him to haul his own ice for the family.

Even though spring was just around the corner the weather remained cold so that old cast iron stove in the kitchen was still being used. It had multiple purposes. A warming oven was situated at eye-level across the top. The cooking area lay below it with a hot water reservoir on the right side and a fire box on the left. A large bake oven was located beneath the cooking area. A coal bucket rested on some newspapers at one side of the stove and a box of firewood with more newspapers occupied the other side. Since there was no gas heater for heat nor for hot water, the iron stove was indeed an important fixture. Mother continued to heat the water for cooking, bathing, doing dishes, and washing laundry on the stove. She looked forward to using the Coleman portable stove again when the weather turned warmer.

The washing machine had been placed in the kitchen, but it would be put on the back porch later. It had to be hand-filled with hot water. It had a pair of rubber rollers which were cranked by hand as wet clothes were fed through them. It was Mother's dream to one day have a new model with automated rollers, even if some early reports had been disastrous. A friend told her that her daughter had leaned over the moving automatic rollers with her long hair and, in the blink of an eye, the rollers grabbed her hair in a vice-like grip and scalped her. Safety equipment would be added in later years, but fingers could also be caught in the rollers and cause excruciating pain.

*View of the row of terraces at Elati Street and West Irvington Place*

One blessing was the radio. It provided the main source of news even though Daddy always read the daily newspaper. The radio also gave joy to the families as they would sit close to it and be entertained by a variety of shows. A favorite was the *Amos and Andy* comedy program starring Freeman Gosden and Charles Forrell when it made its debut on NBS in 1929. The fictitious characters were: "The brassy Kingfish, Amos, Andy, Sapphire, Mama, Calhoun, Madam Queen, Lightnin', and Cousin Leroy." They each had special personalities. As their voices created a story over the air to a large majority of the population, it brought much hilarity at times in a particular setting. This type of entertainment helped many forget some of their problems for a short time.

Naturally, for my parents, one of the most popular was the boxing matches which were described blow-for-blow as the two fighters struggled with all their might for a particular championship. Daddy's fists would curl up and his arms would raise in position for the imaginary punch. It seemed as though part of his heart was still recalling his boxing days. Even though he had good success in his boxing career, he didn't seem to talk much about it.

Another not-to-be-missed event on the radio was when President Roosevelt informed the nation of his current plans to help the economy. Those *fireside chats* were very popular and much needed for the morale of the country.

A favorite and inexpensive pastime was attending baseball games. Denver's up and down history dates back to 1826 with the first recorded game. Colorado produced an astonishing 22 big leaguers during the late 1880s. In the 1890s, no organized team existed in Denver.

In 1900 a team called the Grizzlies was organized in Denver. April 28, 1922 was opening day at Merchants Park located at 600 Broadway. A live bear, exhibited as the team mascot, was firmly secured by ropes as its handlers ran it around the field. Some called the team the Bears after that, and the name stuck.

On October 19, 1927, Babe Ruth lead a team *The Bustin' Babes* against Lou Gehrig's *Larripin Lou's* in an exhibition at Merchants Park. It wasn't until 1930 that electric lights were installed at the park.

Mother and Daddy were avid fans of baseball games and attended often. Edith and I went with them and played underneath the bleachers in the unroofed, open air grandstand. We would have a lot of fun climbing and turning on fence bars and searching for miscellaneous objects hidden about the area. But the best of

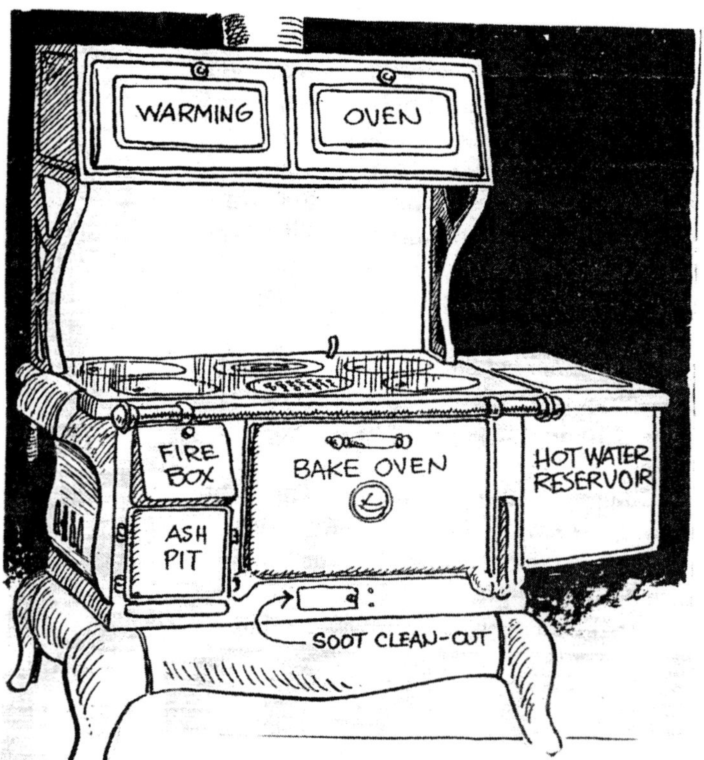


*Cast iron stove used in the kitchen in cold weather*

all was when Daddy would call down to us and give us some money to buy treats. He and Mother usually liked pop and candy, but Edith and I chose crispolettes, a concoction of popcorn, peanuts, and syrup confection molded together. They would last us for a long time.

The Bears did well in 1932-33 with attendance exceeding 5,000 at times, but interest slowly waned. Other Western League members, tired of losing money in Colorado, forced the Bears and the Pueblo Braves out of the league. That killed professional baseball in Colorado for the rest of the decade.

After 1933, semi-pro, amateur and touring teams took center stage. Some of the best baseball came from African-Americans sponsored by local organizations. In 1936, the All-Stars, blessed with pitcher Satchel Page, easily won the Denver Post Baseball Tournament.

It wouldn't be until the 1940s that baseball again prospered in Denver and on August 14, 1948, Bears Stadium opened near West 17th Avenue and Federal Boulevard. Later this became Mile High Stadium. In 1961 seats were added for the opening season of the Denver Broncos Football Club. A further expansion was made to seat 75,000 people in 1968. A unique feature was added in 1977 which allowed for a floating section of the east stands to move hydraulically on a cushion of water to expand the field for baseball.

The entire complex was replaced when Invesco Field at Mile High opened later as the home of the Denver Broncos and newly-built Coors Field became home for the Colorado Rockies baseball team.

One of the main outlets that the communities looked to for entertainment and relaxation was their local theatres. Expanses of comfortable seats and beautifully decorated walls and ceilings were pleasant sights to behold. I have previously reported about the Mayan Theatre. It was one of the two theatres that our family attended regularly. The other was the Webber Theatre at 119 Broadway. It had opened on February 1, 1917 with a 1,000-seat capacity. Both theatres beckoned patrons with special give-away promotions.

Every Saturday afternoon was *go-to-the-show* time for Edith and me. The cost of admittance at both the Mayan and Webber was ten cents for children under twelve years of age, and twenty-five cents for adults. Daddy would always plan to have a few dollars saved for special treats as he handed the money to Mother for the household budget. Money was hard to come by and she was very aware of the unique care needed to make it last until the next

*The "Grizzlies" Baseball Team Opening Day at Merchants Park*

payday. Then, accounting for the absolute necessities of life, she always managed to put aside fifteen cents for each of her little girls. That was Edith's and my allowance for the Saturday matinee at the movies.

As the newly wealthy Edith and me, each with our precious fifteen cents in hand, we would make a mad dash to the nearby Mayan (or Webber). With great anticipation we looked forward to the next Flash Gordon serial. Alas, at the end he was left in some impossible situation. After the newsreel and a cartoon the feature presentation kept us spellbound. With a third of our wealth still intact we managed to select, after much concentration, a five-cent bar of a favorite candy.

As an inducement to part with our money, the Mayan gave away prizes to selected ticket holders. Sometimes a lucky person could walk away with $2.50 in cash. Once a month a grand prize of a bicycle or a Shirley Temple doll was given away. On these afternoons, huge crowds descended upon the theatre to try their luck at such magnificent offerings.

It must have been the *luck of the Irish*. On one occasion Edith and I were attending the Saturday matinee at the Mayan when the grand prize for the month was brought out on the stage for all to see. It was a beautiful black bicycle. With great fanfare, a ticket was drawn from a large barrel container. Edith nervously examined her ticket when the number was read. She sighed, "They missed me by one number!" Hurriedly, she asked me, "What's the number on your ticket?" I can remember holding my ticket in a sweaty hand. It was crumpled and hardly recognizable. I had taken for granted that there was no chance that I could win that bicycle. It was the winning ticket! I ran as fast as I could down the aisle toward the stage. A disappointed and angry boy in the audience yelled out, "It's a dame!"

I was lifted up to the stage. The theatre manager checked my ticket and acknowledged that I was the winner. He rolled the bicycle behind the curtain with me close at hand. It was a boy's bicycle. Looking at my small size and the large bicycle, he asked, "Will your father let you have this bicycle?" I could feel my prize slipping away from me. With a voice as loud as I could muster, I yelled, "Call my daddy! Call my daddy!" Fortunately, when the phone range, Daddy was at home. He jumped into his car and drove immediately to the theatre within minutes. He stood on the stage with the manager who explained that this was a boy's bicycle and it would take at least two weeks or more to trade it for a girl's. Not willing to take a chance, Daddy picked up the bicycle and said to me, "Let's go!"

Daddy placed the bicycle on the front bumper of the car and we three drove home with the precious cargo. For some reason that I could not understand, Daddy's no-nonsense approach to a rather strange situation suited him perfectly. He always seemed to be in complete control.

Edith could ride a bicycle; I could not. We made a deal that if she would teach me how to ride she was then half-owner. Of course, she had to pay her share for any additions or repairs. The deal seemed fair and Mother and Daddy approved. Lessons began by having us both ride at the same time. Edith sat on the seat and had me sit on the bar that extended from the seat to the handle bars. This was the standard design for a boy's bike. A girl's bike did not have this bar and was much easier to get on and off. If I sat on the bar and held onto the handle bars without leaning to my left or right, everything was fine. We lost our balance when I leaned to the opposite direction from which she tried to turn. We had some pretty bad falls before I learned the ropes. That ground can be very hard. No bones were ever broken and, with a lot of practice, we made a good team. Soon she began to let me ride alone. I became quite good, or so I thought, and ventured a few blocks from home where there were streetcar tracks in the middle of the street. As the tires hit the tracks, my bike threw me out of balance and I landed on the ground. That happened only once, and my scrapes and bruises healed fast.

That bicycle became a great joy to Edith and me.

Our family patronized the Webber Theatre also. To gain a competitive edge, both the Mayan and Webber offered their own special inducements for both adults and children. For twenty-five cents an adult could purchase a ticket for the chance drawings. Bank Night was a great favorite and when the theatre was full, people stood outside on the front sidewalk with their tickets in hand. The grand prize was always a monetary award which, if not won, accumulated from week to week, reaching a considerable sum of upwards to one hundred dollars.

On Saturday nights, the theatre manager was quite creative in the selection of tempting prizes. Sometimes this would include a deed to a piece of property to the west of Denver. Small amounts of money, as low as five dollars, or a nice cake were also offered.

One Saturday night, Daddy reached into his pocket and pulled out a few dollar bills that he had been able to save from his paycheck. He knew all too well the value of the dollar. He and Mother agreed that they would enjoy going to the Webber for a night out and a chance to win a prize. They soon found themselves seated in the theatre. After watching the current movie, etc., it was time for the drawings. The first prize was for a pair of lots in Indian Hills west of Denver. The second prize was a beautiful large white coconut cake. Daddy held the winning ticket. The manager confirmed the number as correct and told him that he had just won the first prize of the pair of lots in Indian Hills. Also, unfortunately, a requirement for awarding and then receiving the prize was that the past-due taxes on the property had to be paid. Daddy's resources were already stretched to their limit just to provide for the family, leaving no possibility of scraping together enough money for the taxes. Reluctantly, he had no choice but to decline the offer and the prize. He looked at that white coconut cake and then looked at the manager. He said, "I'll take that white cake instead of the pair of lots in Indian Hills." Mother heaved a sigh of relief; the choice was the right one. Needless to say, we all enjoyed that delicious cake!

Another wonderful win took place when Edith and I were at the Saturday matinee at the Webber. Edith had the winning ticket for the grand prize of a Shirley Temple doll. She was so proud of her new treasure and enjoyed it for many years.

After supper one evening Mother informed Daddy that both Edith and I were in need of new shoes. This was an expense that they had both put off as long as possible. But, they agreed, they could wait no longer. Each of us had only one pair of shoes and they were used for all occasions. And now, the usual mending was to no avail. To cover a hole in the bottom of our shoes a cardboard insert was cut the size of the ball of the foot and then shoved into the shoe. This had been done many times. In inclement weather this temporary fix didn't last long. Both pairs of our shoes were beyond repair. Daddy went to his emergency cash fund and gave Mother the money for the big purchase.

As soon as Edith and I returned home from school that same day, Mother took us to downtown Denver and the May Company Department Store at 16th and Champa Street. It was a favorite place for buying our clothes. Mother made plans to meet friends who also had to do some shopping.

We arrived at an upper floor where there was a large playroom. Both small babies and young children were welcome to use the facilities. A nurse, who was dressed in a proper white uniform with a starched white cap, greeted us all at the door where everyone signed in. She was employed by the store and there was no charge for her services. She provided any service that was needed for all of the little ones. In the middle of the room was a merry-go-round where Edith and I ran to be first on board and to choose our favorite horse. When other children were ready for the ride, it would go round and round with the music playing. There were toys and games to keep us busy. This was a pleasant experience for the mothers. Time could be spent in a no-hassle shopping environment with no chasing little ones around aisles and counters. They all felt that they could safely leave them in good hands. We waved goodbye to Mother as she left the room for the bargain basement.

Sometimes when we weren't left in the nursery we went with her and watched as she made her way through the tables piled high with all kinds of clothing. She would check each piece carefully. The upper floors would send over-stocked merchandise to the basement where the prices were marked down considerably. Some items were soiled or in need of mending and were sold at huge discounts. Indeed, the bargain basement could be quite a treasure trove for our Mother.

Since there was a time limit for the nursery service, Mother made her way to the upper floor to fetch Edith and me. Holding hands, the three of us went to the main floor where the children's shoe department was located. And now, Mother knew what would happen. It was always the same old story. I rushed to the display and my selection was a pair of shiny black patent leather shoes with a black grosgrain ribbon strung through an eyelet on each side of the shoe, tied together and made into a bow. For herself, Edith picked out the same style of shoes. Her little girls loved pretty things, and Mother knew this all too well. Although we were shown other kinds of more sturdy shoes, Edith and I would shake our heads with disapproval. Even though Mother realized that the sturdy shoes were more practical, she gave in. The shoes were to be used for school, play, and dress-up. There was no money for additional kinds of shoes. Mother seemed to have a special intuition that maybe there are times when one cannot be practical. Edith and I proudly carried our precious packages as we left the store. We were very happy little girls.

Returning home, my sister and I could hardly wait to tell Daddy all about our fun experience in the nursery and, above all, to show him the beautiful new shoes. He hugged each of us, grinned and nodded his approval. We were so lucky to have such understanding and loving parents.

Shirley Temple was at the height of her movie career. Tap dancing became extremely popular as she sang and danced her way into the hearts of Americans. It seemed as though every young girl wanted to be like her. Dance studios became popular. Tap dance teachers were sent to some of the grade schools to teach eager students.

I remember running home after school one day and telling Mother that the dance teacher wanted to see her. The next day, Mother appeared in the tap dancing class as I was following the teacher's instructions of "brush-tap-down, brush-tap-down" and other steps. The teacher told her that I would be a good candidate for some professional training. Mother was pleased and told her she would talk to my daddy. There was a dance studio on South Broadway not too far from our home and they decided that, by stretching the budget, they could afford to pay for some lessons for me. That's when my "feeble" dancing career began. Mother would send me each week with a small amount to cover the tap dance lessons. After several weeks a recital was planned. There were about six of us young girls who were to dance together and to wear similar costumes. That meant that Mother had to pay for one to be sewn. How she could stretch that budget again was almost like a miracle. She was determined that I should be included. As a result, our little group performed at the studio and at one of the theatres. It was nothing to brag about!

I was very limber and my dance teacher informed Mother that she wanted me to take adagio lessons. Since Mother could not afford the cost of the extra lessons, the teacher said that she would not charge for them. A strong young boy was introduced to us as my designated partner. Lessons were arranged and my male partner and I practiced an adagio routine. He would throw me around and I would do back-bends and splits. At one of the lessons I was instructed to stand on top of a piano and then, with folded arms, jump into his outstretched arms. It took a lot of coaxing from the teacher to get me to jump. Finally, which I'm sure seemed like an eternity to the teacher, I jumped! I must confess that adagio can be difficult and terrifying at times. When one is tossed up and over your partner's shoulder and then have to slide down his back onto a cold wooden floor, that is really a feat to master!

After many weeks show-time was approaching. Mother had to squeeze the budget again for a special costume for the adagio performance. A seamstress was happy to make it for me. It had a black top with full sleeves dotted with silver sequins. The black satin briefs were designed with a mass of the same sequins in a v-shape on the front. It was indeed a beautiful costume. I do believe the dance was a success. As the final part of the performance took place I was thrown over my partner's shoulders and slid down his back head first and landed in a back-bend. I think I heard some gracious applause from the audience. I suspect that it was mostly from my loving family.

After about a year of dancing, it was evident that I had tired of the physical demands. Mother and Daddy agreed it was time to end the episode. It had been a good experience but not everyone is destined to a career in the dance world. I certainly was not!

Our story cannot be told without mentioning food. Canning fresh fruits was a seasonal job for most housewives. Mother would bring the two-burner portable Coleman stove out of storage and place it on a small table in the kitchen. No longer could the coal stove be used for cooking when the weather became warm. A large kettle was placed on one of the burners of the stove, filled with a mixture of liquid and a choice of peeled and cut fresh fruit such as peaches, pears, cherries, apples, etc. When cooked, the delicious fruit was canned in glass quart mason jars and sealed with a special lid. After they cooled, she would align them on the pantry shelves for future culinary delights.

Milk was an ingredient that Mother used often in her puddings, cakes, and other items. Junket was a popular choice of Edith's and mine. It came in tablet form that was dissolved in hot milk and, when it set, was similar and had the texture of Mexican flan. Sometimes she would add food coloring for an appetizing effect.

A reliable heavy black iron skillet was a necessity for preparing some foods on the Coleman stove. Mother's Sunday treat was fried chicken. Pork chops, beef, fish, rabbit, and pheasant did well cooked in the skillet. It was easily transported in the car to our many mountain outings. Freshly caught mountain trout were cooked to perfection in that black skillet. After cleaning the fish, the heads were always removed so that Mother could put more in the pan. Her recipe was a simple one - just a coating of flour all over the fish and then fried in oil. The skin was always crispy and the flesh cooked just right. They were so delicious that people would remark that one could eat them one after another like popcorn. Sometimes a few fish were packed in ice and taken home from the mountains, but since there was no refrigeration, the ice box was not adequate for long periods of time. Also, the law permitted a limited catch, and the size had to be correct. It was a constant chore to empty the pan underneath the ice box as the water collected from the melting ice.

One of Daddy's favorite lunches was Mother's bologna sandwiches. A metal food grinder was attached to the side of the wooden kitchen table. She would hand-grind boiled eggs, sweet pickles, hunks of bologna and then add a small amount of salad dressing to moisten the mixture. She would pack two sandwiches in his lunch box along with some cookies and fruit and a thermos of milk or coffee. Daddy was very fond of chocolate candy bars and they were included when possible.

Our mountain trips frequently included the Hestons. Since cars had running boards, they would line four of us children along the running board and sit us on an array of large cans when it was time to eat. A blanket tossed on the ground was the usual picnic area for the adults. Wooden tables and benches were not readily available at that time, but the fun of being in those beautiful places running and playing along the rushing clear streams made for many enjoyable times.

And since this section is about food, I must add information on some of the other great menus. Sometimes after treks to the mountains both of the families would meet in North Denver at the Heston's house. It was Grandma Alfrey's house and she had made a home for Aunt Mildred, Uncle Jasper, Jack, Junior, and Dorothy. During those desperate Great Depression days, many families had to join together to survive. Uncle Jasper was employed but his job in an office did not pay a very adequate salary for a family of five.

Grandma Alfrey's ancestors had immigrated from Czechoslovakia so some of the dishes she prepared - and Mother and Aunt Mildred also - were chicken and dumplings and cut-up chicken for soup made with homemade noodles. The noodle dough was first rolled out with a wooden rolling pin in large circles and then hung over the backs of chairs that had been covered with clean dish towels. When the dough was the proper texture, it was placed on a floured board and cut by hand into long rows as close together as possible. The noodles were then dropped into boiling chicken broth until done. The thinner noodles were desired but I personally liked them thicker. What a delicious taste! And, of course, older hens were usually boiled and used for many dishes since they were more inexpensive.

Sauerkraut was popular with dishes of rice and ground beef, spare ribs, and pork hocks. These types of dishes could be made in quantities to feed a large family. Potatoes were often added.

But the crowning glory of all were the kolaches (kolacechs) that Grandma Alfrey would make. (These were mentioned previously.) They were not a bread nor a sweet dough but perhaps something in between. She would catch the nearby streetcar and take it to downtown Denver. There she would get off at a large market in the lower part of town and she would buy poppy seeds. This was one of the special ingredients for one of her rolls. At home, she would crush the poppy seeds and mix them with a thickening of some kind. Then the mixture was cooked on the stove until it was of filling consistency. She prepared seedless prunes in the same manner for filling. After the special dough was

*Grinder that was used for those favorite bologna sandwiches*

ready, she cut the dough in little squares. As she placed a small amount of either the poppy seed mixture or the prune filling in the middle of a square, she would always tell me to "bring up each end to the middle, like a diaper, and pinch it together." She always made dozens of both kinds and kept the families supplied with the most delicious rolls one could ever imagine. What a wonderful grandmother! What wonderful kolaches!

* * *

One day a man with a pretty, small black pony was roaming the neighborhood. For a small fee, he would place a child upon the pony's back and take a picture. Mother knew that the cost of taking pictures was not in their budget so she welcomed this chance to have a picture of Edith and me on that pony. We had just come home for lunch when Mother told us to change our school clothes and put on dressy ones. he cut a long piece of ribbon and fashioned a bow for each of our heads. Then she did a fast fix with the curling iron on our otherwise straight locks. That was indeed a special event for Mother. She was so excited to be able to have that picture taken. She seemed to burst with pride that her daughters looked so pretty sitting on the back of the pony. She could hardly wait for Daddy to return home from work to tell him the news. When he saw the finished picture, he seemed very pleased.

On one occasion I was invited to a girlfriend's birthday party. I had noticed at school that she always wore the same blouse and skirt. But this was not unusual for those times. Edith and I also had limited clothing for school but not to that extreme. My friend's verbal invitation directed a group of her friends to her home since some families could not afford the cost of written invitations.

We all arrived at the specified date and time. As we entered the front door of the small house we stepped directly into the living room. There was no furniture in the room. Her mother appeared and told us to sit on the floor. We all sat with our backs leaning against the walls. Since the floor was cold and hard we sat on our skirts. I had brought a small gift that had been purchased at the local five-and-dime store where there was a large supply of gifts priced at ten cents each. The price was right and that was what most everyone else could afford.

After a couple of games - with no prizes - her mother went to the kitchen and returned with a large dish of sandwiches. They were all the same, made of sliced tomatoes between two slices of very soft white bread. That was a new kind of sandwich for me. The soft bread had absorbed the juice of the tomatoes. I gagged as I tried to eat it while my taste buds rejected the combination. Trying to be very polite, I swallowed the best I could. That was all we had to eat or drink. It was evident that my friend's family was very, very poor. The celebration turned out well and we all laughed and enjoyed each other's company. My friend seemed very happy. She had not been forgotten on her birthday. Love from her mother, and doing what she could for her little girl, filled the daughter's heart with delight.

Years later as I would sit and enjoy my bologna delicacy, I remembered that terrible tomato sandwich. But I also remembered the joy of my friend at her birthday party.

Perhaps a lesson can be learned from this little story. Being thankful for what we have, small or large, is more precious than all the money in the world.

Holidays and birthdays were always celebrated. One year at Easter, eggs were selling at bargain prices. Mother was in her glory and she would never pass up an opportunity like that. She boiled and boiled more and more eggs. She used them in many of her concoctions. We all enjoyed cracking, peeling, and eating the freshly boiled eggs, but Mother was the champion!

Gradually, boils began to appear on Mother's face and neck. Daddy would wait for one to come to a head. Then he would carefully remove the core. Sometimes he would use the top of a glass soda bottle that had been heated in hot water and placed over the boil. This was supposed to help draw out the infection but was very painful for Mother.

One day, Mother was in agony. She could hardly hold her head up and complained of pain on one side of her head. Daddy took her to a doctor on South Broadway where he removed a boil that was on the eardrum. The doctor was convinced that the eggs were causing the boils. Mother stopped eating eggs and gradually the boils ceased. How grateful she was - and all of us - that she didn't have to suffer anymore.

*******************************

Christmas was the most special of times for our family. Daddy always brought home a beautiful large Christmas tree for us to enjoy. Even when my sister and I were toddlers in the South Denver home he made sure that colorful lights were hung and centered just right. Many pretty ornaments were placed on the tree, lots of green and red garlands were strung on the branches, shimmering silver icicles were placed one by one on the tree, and a beloved bright star was arranged at the very top. Daddy made sure that the collection of all of his treasures for the Christmas tree were stored safely at our West Irvington home. Each year the tree and all of its trimmings were displayed in his meticulous manner.

Daddy was a religious man but not a church-going man. He respected the religions of other people. He could worship with a fishing rod in his hand or stand on a mountain top overlooking God's creation. Love of his fellow man and standing up for the weak and down trodden were hallmarks of his very existence. The star on top of the Christmas tree was more than a shiny ornament to him.

I was six years old that Christmas morning during the stark

*Doris and Edith Shirley on the pony 1933*

year of 1933. Edith and I knew that there would not be many packages to open. Our parents had explained that Santa (we already knew about the real Santa) was limited on money to spend. We were all standing in our parents' bedroom. Mother slowly brought forth three boxes. She handed one to Edith and one to me. With pent-up excitement and eager hands we opened our gifts. And there, as I looked down, was the most beautiful doll in the world. Her dress was made of organdy with lace trim on the full skirt. She had a slip and matching panties. Blue glass eyes stared back at me with lids that actually opened and closed. My doll was dressed in pink and Edith's in blue. As we hugged our new treasures, Mother announced that the third box also had a doll. She opened it to show Daddy and us how beautiful it was also. It was for our half-sister, Margaret, and we were told that we would be taking it to her very soon. Daddy was pleased. We knew he always loved and remembered Margaret.

Words cannot describe the pure joy those dolls brought to my sister and me. We played hours on end with them. Edith always loved undressing hers and carefully combing her doll's hair. She would re-curl each lock to perfection. Also, she liked to launder her doll's underwear. I, in turn, was happy to keep mine undisturbed.

During the holidays, Daddy, Edith, and I made a visit to see Margaret. Our father left us to spend the day with her. She was also thrilled to receive her doll since her adoptive parents - who were also her aunt and uncle - could not afford expensive gifts either. Their small white frame house sat on the back of a long lot. A large front yard was planted with flowers and vegetables at appropriate times of the year. Margaret had her own bedroom. Since the house had only one bedroom it looked as if the dining room had been converted for her bedroom. She was always cheerful and glad to see us. She had taken piano lessons and we would gather around the piano as she sang and played for us. Her cute little sayings kept us amused. We always enjoyed our visits with Margaret.

Mother always made sure that Margaret was remembered at all holidays and on her birthday. Her love and consideration for Margaret was admirable.

••••••••••••••••••••••••••••••

Birthday celebrations were great at our house. Mother saved a few coins at a time in a fruit jar that sat on the pantry shelf. She knew it was used only for special occasions. And a birthday celebration came under that category. Ice cream and cake were also on the must list. And, of course, a party was essential. Edith and I were always allowed to invite our friends from school for our celebration. I believe it was my seventh birthday when I invited several friends from my class. When someone could not attend, I just gave their invitation to somebody else. It ended up that more children had been invited than my mother knew about - a lot more! On the big day, a very large number of children arrived at our front door. Mother was quite surprised, to put it mildly. There wasn't much room in the small apartment. But, always able to meet a challenge, she announced that the nearby park was where the party was to take place. After everyone headed to the park, she emptied the fruit jar, ran to the corner store, and purchased additional cake and ice cream.

The party at the park was a great success with games and prizes provided. All of the thanks were to my mother for being so understanding. Not everyone had a special mother like her.

The saga of the biting experience created quite a stir in our family. It all started when Edith and I began to have tiny red, itchy bumps on our bodies. They appeared shortly after we started sleeping in our new downstairs bedroom. The condition was worse in the mornings. To the utter dismay of our parents after searching the room, they found, of all things, bedbugs in our mattress. Mother was fit to be tied as the saying goes. She was always a good housekeeper and it was difficult for her to imagine such a condition in her home. She declared war to get rid of those dreadful bugs.

The following day as Edith and I returned from school, we could see what looked like smoke bellowing out of the windows of our bedroom. Mother stood with neighbors watching as the smoke slowly diminished. There was some talk about *candles* that had been used. Pest control was not discussed at that time. The clotheslines in the parking area were filled with our bedding. Everything had been washed and re-washed. Mother had the mattress stretched on some chairs on the back porch and going over it inch by inch, removed any bugs that wanted to call it their home. That night, Edith and I slept on the floor in the living room. The next day everything was returned to our bedroom and, thankfully, that ended the story of those pesky insects. They were gone and our red bumps from their bites and the itching disappeared. Thank goodness!

Some disturbing and unnerving thing happened to our cousin Jack at this time. He had always been a rather sickly child as I have mentioned before. As a baby his little stomach could not tolerate regular milk so he was raised on goat's milk. He was small and thin but there was always a special twinkle in his eyes and he was so good-natured and loving.

The Heston's home on Xavier Street in North Denver had a wooden sidewalk that led from the back door to the alley. At the end of the sidewalk stood a typical stone ash pit. There was a hole at the top where the hot ashes from the coal stove were dumped. Also, a large metal can with a cover sat on top of the ash pit for garbage. The garbage man drove down the alley and dumped the garbage into his truck. This was the service provided to all of the houses. The ashes were picked up separately by another service truck.

Unfortunately, there was an opening at the bottom of the pit where excess ashes would drop and spread out onto the ground. Those hot ashes sometimes contained small chunks of fiery coal.

One day Jack was playing with his brother, Junior, near the ash pit. Children don't always sense danger and as Jack was running very fast, he stumbled into the hot coals that had spread out on the ground. He fell down with his little hands outstretched. Some of the fiery coals stuck into his flesh and burned him severely. One can imagine the terrible pain that little child went through. His mother, Aunt Mildred, tried to help by running cold water over the hot coals. This of course did not help the skin to heal, so further professional medical treatment was administered in a hospital. It took several years for the scars on his hands and arms to heal but they finally disappeared somewhat as new skin grew over the wounds. And, despite all of this pain and suffering, Jack's sweet disposition and love of life never dimmed.

Another story about my cousin Jack was not so tragic; in fact, it was not tragic. It took place in one of the local theatres. Contests were not limited to adults and occasionally one was held for children. And it was at one of those times that Aunt Mildred took her brood - Jack, Junior, and Dorothy - to the theatre. As the lights went up there was an invitation for children under the age of six to enter a talent contest. Jack was dressed in a white shirt and cute bright red short pants. Aunt Mildred led him to the line where other children awaited their turn. There was little Jack, standing on the stage facing the audience all alone. His mother coaxed him to begin singing. His tiny voice was not too audible but he began to sing: "Ba, ba black sheep have you any wool? Yes sir, yes sir, three bags full." Suddenly in the middle of the third rendition of his song, his little red short pants became wetter and wetter, causing a small puddle to appear at his feet. He kept on singing and finished his song. The audience clapped loudly as he was awarded the first prize. Aunt Mildred was embarrassed but a proud smile appeared on her face. Jack took it all in stride.

(This story was told many times over the years — with great laughter!)

••••••••••••••••••••••••••••••••

Of the three and one-half years that our family lived on West Irvington Place, 1933 was the worst. It was terribly cold that winter as I have written previously. Daddy's bout with whooping cough, living on the undesirable second floor of the apartment house, Mother's effort to keep us all fed on a limited budget and, most of all, the lack of employment for Daddy's profession as a plasterer was at times overwhelming.

And 1933 was etched in the memory of the nation for many reasons. It was considered the worst year of the Great Depression, and by March, 13 million people were reported to be jobless. Every community had its share of human misery. Many of the homeless and destitute were sent to poor farms where they could work on the land for food and lodging. The sleeping accommodations were usually barracks which were built in rows every close together. Many felt that their dignity was being stripped from them but at least they were warm and dry.

Challenges for survival were common in many homes and businesses. Bread and soup lines could be found in most communities. Denver was no exception as local newspapers showed unsmiling eyes telling the story of their hopelessness. For many, courage seemed more and more difficult to maintain, especially on an empty stomach and with no money to buy fuel to warm a house or put food on the table. Milk was still selling for ten cents a quart and a loaf of bread cost eight cents. Average weekly wages were $16.65, contrasted with $24.76 in 1929. Southern tenant farmers tried to live on $5.25 a week for a family of four.

Population statistics for 1933 in Colorado state yearbooks showed 239,058 residents. (By 1940 there were 321,810.)

Building permits in twenty leading Colorado cities listed dollar values of $2,782,412 in 1933, $3,747,310 in 1934, and $11,473,160 in 1936. (By 1940 $17,564,059 dollar values in building permits were issued.)

The economic chart continued downward during the winter of

1933. Piecemeal federal and state relief programs were unable to alleviate the growth of suffering among the destitute.

Franklin Delano Roosevelt took his first oath of office as President of the United States of America on March 4, 1933. Economic activity in the state of Colorado had almost staggered to a halt. Agriculture braced itself for another year of drought and farm prices continued to fall. Trade faltered with bank failures, currency hoarding, and a general climate of restricted business activity. Mining had come to a virtual standstill. Summer tourism had not yet begun. Perhaps one out of every five employable individuals were out of work.

The President promised a *New Deal* that would develop a variety of programs aimed at joblessness, unemployment insurance, old-age pensions, welfare programs, wage, hour, and child labor laws. Also, he asked for laws that would encourage labor organizations and collective bargaining.

Many events and changes were about to happen.

On top of President Roosevelt's list of priorities in 1933 were the many problems that faced our nation's banks. Most were closed or in serious trouble. Of the 174 banks in Colorado, 56 closed between 1929 and 1933. The President ended depositors' runs on banks by closing all of them. In a special session of Congress on March 9, 1933, only those banks in a sound condition were allowed to reopen. In June, through the Glass-Steagall Act, the Federal Deposit Insurance Corporation (FDIC) was approved, guaranteeing deposits and providing additional stability to the economy.

More than half of America's elderly citizens lived in poverty in reports that dated back to 1929. The President was quoted as saying:

*No greater tragedy exists in modern civilization than the aged, worn-out worker who after a life of ceaseless effort and useful productivity must look forward for his declining years in a poorhouse. A modern social consciousness demands a more humane efficient arrangement.* (The Social Security Act was not approved by Congress until 1935.)

In May of 1933, Congress authorized the President to appoint a board of three directors for the Tennessee Valley Authority (TVA). It was established to provide flood control and cheap hydroelectric power for one impoverished region of the country. This was only one of the board's many important functions.

The Truth in Securities Act of 1933 and an act that established the regulatory Securities and Exchange Commission (SEC) in 1934 offered some promise.

Roosevelt proposed legislation to legalize beer with 3.2% alcoholic content. By December 1933, the 21st Amendment had been ratified, repealing the 18th Amendment regarding prohibition.

In 1934, Daddy was still working for Watkins, but he expressed to Mother that at times he was looking forward to getting back to his plastering trade. He never gave up hope that things could get better. He became more and more active in his Plasterers and Cement Finishers Union. He attended all of the evening meetings. There was a feeling in the air that something was happening. It seemed as though the worst year of 1933 was over.

More changes were beginning in 1934 in our country and this included Denver, Colorado and the labor movement. With the many welcome new federal projects that had created needed jobs, construction work was now beginning to be on the move. One of the most popular and constructive of the New Deal programs in 1934 was the Civilian Conservation Corps (CCC). Eventually more than 3.4 million young men, ages 17 to 25 and unmarried, served in all forty-eight states, the territories of Alaska and Hawaii, Puerto Rico, and the Virgin Islands. The standard pay for an enrollee was thirty dollars a month. Many sent a large portion home to help their families. Almost three billion trees were planted. Enrollees also served as firefighters and protected and improved parks and campgrounds. Trails and roads were built. They strung telephone lines and restored an estimated 3,900 historic structures.

Since the CCC was specifically for unemployed young men, they lived in camps while they worked in state and national parks to help preserve timber and soil resources. When appropriate, they also received other training such as learning to read and write. Colorado had numerous CCC camps throughout its undeveloped forested lands.

Red Rocks Park and Amphitheatre, once known as the Garden of the Angels, was built between May, 1936 and June, 1941 by the CCC.

Another CCC project was the Saddlehorn Caretaker's House and Garage at the Colorado National Monument near Fruita built in 1935 and 1936. They were the first permanent buildings at the monument. The Saddlehorn Comfort station was also built by the CCC in 1937 to accommodate the recreational needs of visitors to the monument.

The 1930s witnessed the passing of several labor laws. One

was the Railway Labor Act of 1934. Another was one of the most important of the Roosevelt administration's New Deal labor legislation, the National Labor Relations Acts (NLRA) of 1935, usually called the Wagner Act. The following consists of partial quotes from the Act:

*... Section 7 guaranteed employees the right to self organization - to bargain collectively through representatives of their own choosing, and to engage in concerted activities for the purpose of collective bargaining or other mutual aid or protection.*

*Section 8 set forth five unfair labor practices of employers which were to be prohibited. (1) interference with attempts by employees to form and join independent unions; (2) fostering, domination and control of dependent unions; (3) discrimination such as discharge, against employees because of their interest in unions, with a proviso that discharge for refusal to join a union under a valid closed - or union - shop contract was privileged - a closed shop being one in which anyone may be hired, although everyone must join the contracting union to retain his job; (4) retaliation against employees for testifying or participating in proceedings under this act; and (5) the refusal to bargain in good faith with the union representing the employer's workmen.*

Early in 1937 the Supreme Court declared the Wagner Act valid. For the first time, Congress and state legislatures seemed free to regulate by law the relationship between employers and employees.

It wasn't until 1938 that the Fair Labor Standards Act was enacted and upheld by the Supreme Court with provisions for "minimum hourly wage, a maximum work week of 40 hours with a penalty of time and one-half for weekly overtime, child labor restrictions and regulation of homework and sweated labor." It also included sanctions against employers who violated the act "... criminal prosecutions, injunctions and recovery by underpaid employees of double payment, with costs of litigation assessed against the employer."

Another widespread relief program to help the unemployed was the Works Progress Administration (WPA) which was founded in 1935 for large public works projects such as roads and dams. Part of the WPA was a program begun on October 4, 1937 to convert the grounds of the former Agnes Memorial Sanatorium into a modern airfield. This became Lowry Field and in 1947 was renamed Lowry Air Force Base.

The Salida Hot Springs Pool, Colorado's largest indoor hot springs, was built in 1937 by the WPA. The project employed about 200 men for digging and laying the original pipeline and constructing buildings.

Both the CCC and the WPA built Land's End Road, Forest Service No. 100, a 12-mile spur of the Grand Mesa Scenic Byway. Also, the Land's End Observatory, built in the 1930s, which sits on the rim of the Grand Mesa and has views extending to the La Sal Mountains in Utah as well as other southern ranges, was the combined effort of the CCC and the WPA.

One of the most successful of early projects established in 1936 was the Public Works Administration (PWA). By 1936, PWA completed forty federal projects in Colorado. A huge water diversion system was begun to bring west slope water to east slope customers. The Moffat Water Tunnel was the first Colorado request of the PWA. In January 1934, it was overwhelmingly approved and work began in early 1935. It was completed in late 1938 at a cost of 9.5 million dollars. (*The Denver Post*, 1933, 1934, 1935.)

Another large-scale PWA project, initiated in the late 1930s, was the Grand Lake Diversion Plan, later called the Colorado Big Thompson Projects. This undertaking was the fourth largest irrigation project in the nation involving a network of water collection points on the western slope, five major dams, a 13-mile tunnel under the Continental Divide, five hydroelectric power plants, and storage reservoirs on the western slope. Its purpose was to provide eastern slope farmers with abundant irrigation water and to produce more electricity than all of Colorado was then consuming. Contracts began in late 1937 (Bureau of Reclamation, 1953). (From *Colorado Year Book*, 1948-1950, pp. 263-266. Also *Colorado Magazine*, January 1953).

Other Denver-area construction and improvement PWA projects were sewage disposal plants, Fitzsimons Hospital, the State Capitol Annex, and the Army Air School at Lowry Air Field.

The year 1934 began to show some economic recovery. The labor movement in Denver welcomed new federal projects and the subsequent creation of needed jobs. Construction work slowly awakened from the doldrums. All crafts and skills were needed.

This was the time when Daddy left his Watkins job in favor of returning to his plastering trade. He was grateful that he had been employed by such a very reliable and honest company. Memories of dealing with kind customers on his route were always with him. But now the telephone range more frequently with calls from his

Pa notifying him of new building projects needing qualified plasterers and cement finishers. Government buildings and new homes prodded the early movement forward.

Very early each morning Daddy left to go to work. Mother packed his favorite bologna and egg sandwiches in his lunch bucket along with whatever she knew he liked. He was a big man with a healthy appetite and needed all the fuel he could muster. His work day was a very long one -- commonly twelve hours, six days a week. Workmen still received no health benefits, no paid vacations, no over-time, and low wages. (Editor's note: the Fair Labor Standards Act would not be passed for another three years.)

In the evening when Daddy returned home after a long day of plastering, the same routine took place as before he had the Watkins job. Mother boiled water on the Coleman stove and helped carry buckets of water up to the second floor bathroom. Sometimes, after he had soaked in the soothing water, she would rub his shoulders with a favorite Watkins product - a liniment.

I can remember when Daddy discussed the work schedule that was expected of him and all of the other tradesmen. As a plasterer, he frequently had only a week's time to prepare the interior walls of a small five-room house. Wooden strips were first nailed to the stone walls by other workmen, then lath strips of metal were attached with special nails. Lathers covered corners and other surfaces in preparation of the first coat of brown *mud* which was usually hand-mixed and waiting in a wheelbarrow. The mud was slung on with a trowel very quickly. The time element was very critical. It was essential that the walls be ready for the finished white plaster coating. Again, white plaster was hand-mixed in a large metal rectangular trough and applied with a trowel. This was the art of plastering that was so unique. The eye of the plasterer followed the movement of the wet plaster as the trowel moved back and forth, making a wall straight and true. Daddy said that there was no such thing as a 100% result in measurement, but the naked eye could not detect anything but the marvel of a finished plastered wall. He could also create a perfectly formed archway between rooms when it was so desired, and make artistic molds with designs that were used in ceilings with light fixtures. He worked on some of Denver's churches and other public buildings that required special plaster work. (Author's Note: If some of the description of the plaster work has flaws it is the fault of the author. In later years, I observed my father plastering in the basement of my first home with the help of my husband.)

In spite of the long working hours, Daddy seemed to have time and the energy to attend his union meetings. Also, there were visits with his fellow workers and friends in our home. Even though Edith and I were young girls at the time, we knew that a lot of important activity was going on. We were too busy with our schooling and having fun just being girls to know the implications of those moments for the labor movement. But even at our tender ages, we began to note a more serious tone in the conversations of our parents. Mother and Daddy were discussing job-related issues more and more. They agreed that the working man should have shorter working hours and better security and that a man alone had no voice. It was reported that Daddy had become more and more outspoken at the Union Hall about his opposition to the treatment of his fellow workers. Some members reported that their bosses were demanding longer working hours and even lower wages at the price of continued employment.

Male friends of Daddy's who were also involved with the Union were very loyal to his actions and supported him in every way they could. Two of his favorite friends were Carl and Ed. Carl was a large, burly, no-nonsense man who physically helped out at the union meetings if things got out of control. And out of control they did get at times, according to reports brought home. If the rowdiness became too disruptive, usually by hecklers in the back of the meeting hall, it was told that Daddy would leave his position at the podium and walk directly to the trouble-makers and instigators looking for a fight and, with Carl's support, the rowdy ones were taken care of nicely and quickly. And Ed, who was in the boxing game the same time as Daddy, was always there to lend a hand. They mused that their boxing backgrounds seemed to come in handy when needed.

Some evenings provided time for Daddy to study American history which was seemingly a favorite topic for him. He had a ferocious appetite for more knowledge about his country and seemed to enjoy many hours of reading. The favorite set of large reference books were well used and the daily newspaper was a must for him to read. He studied and read all articles about current events and those relating to the working man. He voiced his own opinions spontaneously. He would explain to Mother what was wrong and what should be done to help his fellow man. This sincerity and special energy began to make him popular in the labor movement and most of the fellow members of his union began to support him and his positions.

The Plasterers and Cement Finishers Union, Local No. 32, Denver, Colorado, looked for new leadership to move them forward. They found such a leader — a man of strength, one who understood the needs of the working man, and the ability to take the labor movement forward. That leader was my father, James W. Shirley.

Daddy was humbled by the trust and responsibility placed upon him and proved this was one of those times that a very special individual was made to be a true leader of men. He was not only built for the job with his boxing background, but his sincere convictions were apparent to his fellow workers. With his qualifications and professional appearance he was overwhelmingly nominated to become their new president.

And now, one of the most important decisions of his life had to be made. He was asked to run for the office of President of his Union. It would be a full-time job that would not only put him in a position of power to negotiate with contractors and businessmen, but it would also put him in dangerous and risky situations. Although unions were becoming stronger, anti-labor objectors were growing at an equal rate. Clashes and violent behavior were becoming commonplace.

Lengthy discussions between Daddy and Mother took place. Agreement was made that he would run for the office.

It was unanimous. My father was elected President of the Operative Plasterers and Cement Finishers International Association, Local No. 32, 1934.

There were many labor laws passed - some protecting the employer - but those passed in the 1930s were the very basic ones for the rights of the working man, and that is what the new Colorado labor leader believed in and acted upon. He stated that:

*Every man - no matter what color he is - has the right to work for a decent home and provisions for his family - a decent way of life. After all, the craftsman provides his fellow man with protection from the elements. ~ James W. Shirley, 1934*

To rise above all odds in a terrible time during the Great Depression, my father, James W. Shirley, earned my title of

HERO OF WEST IRVINGTON PLACE

CHAPTER VII

# A LIFE WELL LIVED

The school year was over for Edith and me in June, 1936. It was time for our family to move from West Irvington Place to our home at 1117 South Columbine Street in south Denver. Many memories were left behind for all of us and most were happy ones in spite of Mother and Daddy having to cope with the many changes brought about in the Great Depression. They survived. Daddy's new, enlarged affiliation with the unions made life financially better, while fulfilling his dream of doing something he was very excited about - being part of the growing labor movement.

As we settled into our home once again it was a joy to have use of those conveniences that were not available on West Irvington Place. Having natural gas connection meant automatic hot water available from a large tank. The water faucets actually produced hot water on demand. And there was a bathtub for all to enjoy. What a wonderful luxurious experience to stretch out and soak in it! After sharing a small wash tub, this was like a gift from God. Gas for the stove in the kitchen and a coal furnace in the basement that heated the entire house added considerably to our comfort level.

Since we lacked a dining room set, that was the first purchase Daddy made. He found a large table with matching chairs at a second hand store. There was no need for a buffet as one was already built in the room. This furniture was a real necessity since the breakfast nook gave way to a new refrigerator - one that made real ice cubes!

By the fall of 1936, Edith and I returned to Washington Park

Elementary School and resumed our studies. Apparently some classes were overcrowded and we were given several written and oral tests to determine our progress. As a result of the testing, we both skipped a grade. Our parents were delighted and Edith and I fared well at our beloved school.

By this time, Daddy's career began to boom. There was a demand for expertise in labor organizing. He continued serving as business agent for the Plasterers' and Cement Finishers' Union, Local No. 32, as well as working for the American Federation of Labor as an organizer for the Operating Engineers, Local No. 5. The year 1936 was an active year for both Mother and Daddy in their lives as part of the expanding labor movement.

By 1937, Mother and her best friend, Suzie Walsh, organized the first Women's Auxiliary for the Operative Plasterers' and Cement Finishers' International Association, Local No. 32, Denver, Colorado. Mother was President and Suzie Walsh was Vice-President. The twenty ladies in the picture are wives of union members. They helped raise funds for many worthwhile causes. One of the jobs that Mother especially liked was going to businesses to solicit donations of prizes for the activities of Labor Day. And, indeed, Labor Day became the highlight of the fall season in Denver.

A little previous history of Labor Day reveals that the very first Labor Day Parade was on September 5, 1882 in New York City. Labor leaders envisioned a festive day and a parade through the streets of New York to pay tribute to American workers. They chose the first Monday in September when weather was generally pleasant. Ten thousand workers, led by a brass band, marched around Union Square and up Fifth Avenue to 42nd Street. An afternoon picnic and an evening dance with a fireworks display topped off the day.

Over the years, Labor Day grew in popularity as other cities and states began to adopt the traditions of parades and picnics. In 1887, five states, including Colorado, passed legislation recognizing Labor Day as a legal holiday. On June 28, 1894, Congress declared the first Monday of September a national holiday.

Labor Day was the last big day of excitement and fun before school began each year in the 1930s and 1940s. At that time there were two amusement parks in northeast Denver - Elitch Gardens and Lakeside Amusement Park. Elitch's had many beautiful flowers, rides, a theatre, roller coaster, dance hall, and other amenities. Lakeside was a co-favorite. It had opened in 1908 as Lakeside Amusement Park and was originally known as White City. It was located at what is now I-70 and Sheridan Boulevard and was still operating in 2009. Elitch's, originally at 38th and Tennyson, closed several years earlier and moved to the downtown area under new ownership. Lakeside's Cyclone roller coaster was built in 1940 and was always a favorite ride even though its jerky, clanking ascent to the first big fall could make you feel that the 90-second ride would be over fast - very fast! The park boasted a little train that took its passengers on a bumpy ride on its tracks around the park. There was a penny arcade where, after you inserted a penny in a slot, a view-box flipped through some rather naughty pictures. It was popular, to say the least. The fun-house was a delight to explore and a hidden employee would blow air through holes in the floor and make the girls' skirts go up into the air. That was popular with the boys. It had mammoth slides. One went straight down. If you didn't hold your bare arms beside your body, it would burn your flesh like the very dickens. Also, a merry-go-round, indoor swimming pool, and a dance hall that overlooked a lake were some of the unique places to enjoy at Lakeside.

Something that interested all of the children was the *Nickel Man*. He was somewhat akin to a mystery man in that nobody knew who he was. He would roam the grounds like a mysterious ghost. His only quest was to give away a free nickel. And a nickel at that time was worth having. On one occasion, we were in front of a small white frame eatery and it was rumored that Nickel Man had made his mark by secretly handing out that special coin. Still, no one knew what he looked like. A large crowd gathered, hoping someone new would be a winner. I was getting tired of waiting and went by myself to a bench near the merry-go-round for a rest. As I was looking at the scenery I suddenly felt something hard and cold pressed into my left hand. Before I could see what happened, the invisible Nickel Man had done his job. There it was! A shiny nickel looking up at me in my left hand! I became the envy of the other children. Happiness can indeed raise its beautiful head in strange ways.

And now, that very special Labor Day in September, 1937 arrived. In downtown Denver the parade left Civic Center at 8:00 a.m. and would last for almost an hour. In their own specified groups walking the entire route, the participants consisted of plumbers, glaziers, carpenters, painters, electricians, postal workers, steamfitters, roofers, laborers, bricklayers, cement finishers, plasterers, printers, firemen, asbestos workers, sleeping car porters, etc. At the very front of the parade was the Grand Marshall, my Daddy, James W. Shirley, wearing a large beautiful identifying badge. I can still see him in my mind as he walked briskly and proudly with his head held high, all alone, leading his beloved workers. He would repeat this honor again the next year in 1938.

On one occasion, as he neared the grandstand, Mother, Edith, and I waited patiently to see him advancing. Prior arrangements had been made so that I could run out and be with him for a few blocks. Being shy, Edith didn't want to march with him, but I did. And there he was, in sight, marching at a steady, fast parade pace. I sprinted out of the stands and joined him. I can remember his hand grasping mine in a loving and protective way as I struggled to keep up. After a short march, I returned to the grandstand. The parade continued to upper 14th Street and back to Colfax Avenue where it ended. With great anticipation we looked forward to the afternoon at Lakeside which was to follow.

*First Women's Auxiliary 1937* *Suzie Walsh - Mary Shirley*

The union members and their families made plans to meet at Lakeside. When they all finally arrived they found wonderful treats. The unions had contributed to furnishing free ride tickets, ice cream, pop, beer, watermelon, and an assortment of breads, salads, and lunch meats and cheeses for sandwiches. What an abundance of food - all you could eat and drink.

After lunch an announcement was made that the games would soon begin for both adults and children, with prizes for the winners. Some of the events were similar to those our family had attended at other picnics. Mother and Aunt Mildred entered their usual kick-the-shoe contest with dismal results. Edith and I entered the foot races and were lucky to both win prizes.

One of the more interesting contests was the one to find out who was wearing the most union labels (fondly referred to as *Union Bugs*) on their clothing. It was a male event only. Since underwear was included, the participants were reminded that modesty was the best policy and they would not have to show that item of clothing. Daddy and his friends had a big time teasing one another over the rules. Since Daddy was always a great kidder, one can imagine what went on. When the final tallies were counted, one of the dedicated and proud union members walked off with his prize. The Union Label was an important trademark. It showed that the item of clothing and other products such as printing, cigars, personal products, etc., were made by union members.

And then the most important and valuable prize of all was revealed. It was displayed in all of its shiny beauty on an elevated stand - a new car! Tickets had been sold for several weeks previously by most of the unions to help pay for this expensive grand prize. All of the stubs had been put in a large container, mixed thoroughly, and only one ticket was drawn. As the winning ticket for the car was announced, a hushed silence hung over the crowd. Then the sound of a very excited voice rang out loudly - it was the lucky winner! Everyone had a great time.

*Grand Marshal 1937 badge*

*Grand Marshal 1938 badge*

*Headband for Straw Hat*

## BADGES

**1937**

Operative Plasterers & Cement Finishers International Assn, 29th Biennial Convention, September 13, 1937, Baltimore, Maryland.
Gold medallion delegate badge, hanging from purple satin ribbon, shows figures in century-old costumes holding shovel and tool with Latin inscriptions.

LABOR DAY, fall of September, 1937, Denver, Colorado
Grand Marshal, very large red, white and purple round badge at top with gold fringe and purple satin ribbon below with gold tassels.

31st Annual Convention, Building and Construction Trades Department, A.F. of L. Denver, Colorado, September 29, 1937.
Delegate badge, silver medallion with "American Federation of Labor, Org. Nov. 15 1881" with hands clasped in center of world, hangs from purple satin ribbon.

57 Annual Convention, American Federation of Labor, Denver, Colorado, October 4 - 16, 1937.
Three badges - two silver metal and one gold metal
The two silver ones show "Vice Chairman of Conv. Comm," and the other "Guest." The gold one shows "Delegate." All three are intricately carved with scene of Denver - the capitol with trees and buildings. There is a burro on the left and a man on horse on the left. Also, all three have a metal shield hanging below showing hands clasped in center of world with American Federation of Labor Orgd. Nov. 15, 1881.

**1938**
43rd Annual Convention the Colorado State Federation of Labor, Colorado Springs, Colorado, June 20, 21, 22, 1938.
Gold satin ribbon hangs from yellow metal badge.

LABOR DAY, fall of September, 1938, Denver, Colorado
Grand Marshal, same as 1937 badge except for "GRAND MARSHAL" in top center of the badge is red rather than purple.

LABOR DAY COMMITTEE hat bands for straw hats, 1936, 1937, and 1938.

**1939**

44th Annual Convention, The Colorado State Federation of Labor, Pueblo, Colorado, June 19, 20, 21, 1939.
Lavender satin ribbon hangs from lavender metal badge.

American Federation of Labor, Western States Conference, Salt Lake City, Utah, December 16th and 17th, 1939. Gold metal bracket holds name of delegate with a purple satin ribbon hanging beneath.

Thirtieth Convention, O.P. & C.F.I.A. (Operative Plasterers' and Cement Finishers' International Association), DIAMOND JUBILEE, Denver, Colorado, September 11, 1939.
Three badges - Delegate, Office, and Guest. One is in gold metal and the other two are in copper. They all have the Denver skyline engraved at the top where the name of the person is identified. Below shows cavalry on horse with "let'er buck Denver" engraved. Two have a purple satin ribbon hung below, and one has a blue satin ribbon hung below.

Seventeenth Annual Convention New Mexico State Federation of Labor, Carlsbad, New Mexico, September 15, 16, 17, 1939.
Gold bracket at top holds name of delegate. A blue satin ribbon hangs from that with a round medallion engraving showing an internal view of the cavern with "Carlsbad Caverns" engraved below.

**1940**

45th Annual Convention, The Colorado State Federation of

Labor, Alamosa, Colorado, June 17, 18, 19, 1940.
Ivory satin ribbon hangs from an ivory-colored round badge.

Eighteenth Annual Convention, New Mexico State Federation of Labor and American Federation of Labor, Clovis, New Mexico, September 27, 28, 29, 1940. Two badges with gold bracket at top for names of Delegate and Guest. Hanging from a green satin ribbons, both round medallions depict a picture of a farm with a pig on the left and a ram on the right under an apple tree.

Fifth Western Conference of Teamsters, Albany Hotel, Denver, Colorado, September 1-5, 1940.
Two badges, both with gold metal bracket depicting engraved skyline of Denver at top. Lower portion depicts a cowboy on a bucking bronco. A dark blue satin ribbon hangs from the metal badge.

**1941**
59th Annual Convention Minnesota State Federation of Labor, Minneapolis, Minnesota, September, 1941.
Two badges in the shape of an Indian arrowhead - one silver and one gold engraved with scene of International Falls. One for Delegate; one for Guest.

46th Annual Convention Colorado State Federation of Labor, Greeley, Colorado, June 16-18, 1941. Red, white and blue satin ribbon is hung from ivory-colored medallion.

**1942**
47th Annual Convention Colorado State Federation of Labor,

Colorado Springs, Colorado, June 15-17, 1942.
Dark blue satin ribbon hangs from white medallion showing two American flags in the center.

83rd Annual Convention Nebraska State Federation of Labor, Beatrice, Nebraska, September 14, 15, 16, 1942.
At top, a gold bracket holds name of representative and whom he represents. A red, white and blue satin ribbon hangs below. A gold medallion in an octagon shape hangs from the ribbon. "Nebraska" is engraved in the center with "Nebraska State Federation of Labor" around the edge.

**1945**

Golden Anniversary Colorado State Federation of Labor, 1896-1945, Denver, Colorado, October 19, 20, 21, 1945.
Two gold medallion delegate badges hang from yellow grosgrain ribbon.

**1946**

51st Annual Convention, Pueblo, Colorado, June 13,14,15, 1946.
Two gold medallion delegate badges hang from ivory-colored satin ribbon.

33rd Annual Convention, Colorado State Council of Carpenters, Pueblo, Colorado, June 16, 1946.
At top, a gold bracket holds the name of the representative and whom he represents. A red, white and blue satin ribbon hangs below.

10th Biennial Convention, United Slate, Tile and Composition Roofers Damp and Waterproof Workers Ass'n, Denver, Colorado, September 16, 1946.
At top is a silver engraving of Denver's Capitol with trees and buildings. The name of the representative is in the center. Hanging from that is an ivory-colored satin ribbon. Hanging below the ribbon is a round engraved medallion depicting a large building with figures working on the roof and underground.

32nd Convention O.P. & C.F.I.A. (Operative Plasterers' & Cement Finishers' International Association), Pittsburgh, Pennsylvania, September 9-14, 1946.
At top is a gold bracket engraved with "Organized 1864" in the center. There is a place for the name of the representative. A gold-colored satin ribbon hangs below. Hanging from the ribbon is a gold medallion with Pittsburgh engraved on the top, a seal of the city, and in the background there is an industrial scene.

**1947**

National Conference of Union Labor Legionnaires, Los Angeles, California, 1947. Red, white and blue ribbon hangs from a plastic holder for the name and residence of the delegate.
The next day would be a school day for school-age children and a workday for most of the adults.

Memories of that Labor Day Parade and picnic would remain with many for the rest of their lives, as they will with me.

1937 was the beginning of numerous conventions and meetings. As part of Daddy's responsibilities it was necessary for him to be present as a delegate and participate in the business at hand. Pictures of some of the badges that were worn at these conventions are shown on attached pages. The engravings on some are quite remarkable. Some were supplied by Bastian Bros. Co., a union-run company in Rochester, New York. A small card was found among some of the badges from that company which read:

*A convention badge is more than a means of identifying the wearer as a member of your organization in convention. After the business sessions and entertainments are over it is often the only tangible memento of the meeting. In years to come, it will recall the pleasure of the convention and the friendships made or renewed at it.*

Mother accompanied Daddy to most of the conventions and was provided with proper identification as a guest on her badges.

When our parents were away, Grandma Alfrey came to be with us. She was always teaching Edith and me something new such as how to sew and to embroider. I learned how to iron by watching her as she carefully moved the iron over each piece of clothing. It took time and skill to produce a properly finished item. She was the reason I loved to iron all my life -- much to the bewilderment of many who believe it to be an unpleasant chore. As Edith and I grew older and became more and more involved in school work and other activities, our next door neighbors on each side made sure that we were cared for when our parents were away.

Pictures of some of Daddy's involvement in his job as a labor organizer are shown on some following pages. The old saying "a picture is worth a thousand words" fits very well.

*1937 and 1938 convention badges*

*1939 convention badges*

*1940 convention badges*

*1941 and 1942 convention badges*

*1945 and 1946 convention badges*

*1947 convention badge*

Travel by auto for Daddy's work took our family of four to others parts of the country. We spent short periods of time in Portland, Oregon; Spokane, Washington; Los Angeles, California; Minneapolis, Minnesota; and Albuquerque, New Mexico.

In 1938 and 1939 Edith and I attended 7th and 8th grades at Byers Junior High School in Denver. We did, however, go with Mother and Daddy when he was assigned to organizing at out-of-state locations during our school year. When this occurred, they talked to the principal of the school. They were informed that if Edith and I would attend school in each of the new towns for a reasonable length of time we would not be held back a grade. Thus we enjoyed three months of schooling in Minneapolis, one month in Los Angeles, and a full year in Albuquerque. Those were interesting times and we were happy to be with our parents.

One of the trips to the West Coast was in the summer of 1939. Daddy had business in Los Angeles. He had read about two bridges that had been completed in San Francisco. I can remember how excited he was to see them. Rather than driving directly to Los Angeles, we took a northern route to California.

In 1933, work had begun in San Francisco on the two big suspension bridges. The double-decked Transbay bridge (known locally as the Bay Bridge), designed by C.H. Purcell is four and one-fourth miles long. The huge Golden Gate Bridge, designed by J.B. Strauss, had a span of 4,200 feet across the entrance to the harbor and was the longest span yet built. They were both completed by 1937.

The 1939 Golden Gate International Exposition was celebrating the opening of the bridges and we were fortunate to be able to attend the exhibits. What a wonderful experience to cross the Golden Gate Bridge and behold this amazing engineering marvel of such size and complexity.

One of my favorite memories of the Exhibition was the medical pavilion. It featured new surgical techniques performed by using molds. One was of a person who had lost part of his jaw bone (the mandible) and the shoulder bone (the scapula) was used to replace it. Step by step in special molds, a part of the scapula was removed and lifted up to the missing mandible area as a transplant. I was truly mesmerized by the procedure.

Another memory was of standing in front of a large billboard advertising Sally Rand. She was known for her graceful and almost-nude performances. It was prominently displaying "nude" girls standing behind a large wooden fence with two delicately-placed slats to tantalize the imagination without totally destroying the sense of misplaced modesty. For a twelve-year-old, it looked rather weird to me.

We stopped and ordered ice cream cones at one of the booths. When Daddy was told what the price was - there were no prices advertised anywhere - he told the man to "keep them!" We all walked away. That's a good example that Daddy was never one to let anybody take advantage of him or his family. There were always those who tried but their efforts were put to an end quickly and firmly.

It was time to travel on to Los Angeles. A small apartment was found and Edith and I were enrolled in a nearby school. Mother's first unpleasant encounter was with the water. She said that when she began taking a shower the water smelled like rotten eggs. She was used to good water at home in Denver; it was a shock to her. Bottled water had to be purchased for drinking and cooking.

It was a pleasant time when we visited Uncle John and Aunt Mary in their home. Uncle John had made wise investments in real estate. He had purchased undeveloped property in a large Los Angeles area. Home building boomed and filled the many blocks that he owned. He and Aunt Mary now lived in one of the lovely two-story houses on the very property he named *Prince Square.* He also named some of the streets after family members such as John Street, Mary Avenue, etc. As expected, they treated us with kind hospitality.

*Union Officials - convention and date unknown*

Our schooling was acceptable for Edith and me. The outdoor ramps that led to some of our classes were different from what we were used to but we found them comfortable in the California sunshine. The month passed quickly and it was time to return to Colorado. We packed our belongings in the car and headed for home.

Shortly after we returned to Denver, Daddy received news that he was needed for labor organizing in New Mexico and Albuquerque was to be the home base. We arrived there in the summer of 1940.

A small upstairs apartment was found near a park a couple of blocks away and a hospital was just across the street. It was also within walking distance to the main part of town. Daddy had an office nearby and Mother helped him keep records. There were many towns in which Daddy was assigned to help organize.

In the meantime, Edith and I had fun swimming and enjoying the warm summer months before the first of September when we had to return to school. Edith was now in the 10th grade and was registered to go to Albuquerque High School. I was taken several blocks away, over the desert, to Lincoln Junior High School for the 9th grade. Mother walked with me to the front entrance of the school as other students watched. They were mostly Spanish-Americans and a little curious of me.

As we settled in our new home we looked forward to living in New Mexico. Albuquerque was not as large as Denver, the food was different, and the weather not as severe. Daddy found nice restaurants that prepared good Mexican food which, I believe, we all began to enjoy. Edith was gaining new friends at her school and I was getting acquainted with friendly boys and girls I met while walking to school and in the classrooms. We had excellent teachers. I took my first year of Spanish and found that it took a lot of basic learning. I can honestly report that the one year our family spent in Albuquerque was a highlight of my life. A group of us girls had fun socially after school. I joined a square dance team and the boys made it even more enjoyable. Edith also came home with lots of tales of how much fun she was having at school. She was even allowed to have a few dates.

The following summer, Edith and I looked forward to swimming. On our first day at the pool we luxuriated in the hot, bright sun. When we returned home, Mother was worried about us. Our fair skins had turned into a bright red and we were so warm that she feared we were running a temperature. We could not stand to have any clothing rubbing on the burned skin. She and Daddy found some cream for us to spread on our skin which seemed to help some. Since we could not go out, we spent all the time in the apartment. As the healing took place, we took turns peeling off the old skin. We had a contest to see who could peel off the largest piece. I stored a piece in a drawer and later found it had shrunk. What goofy things young girls can do! We did not know at that time how damaging too much sun can be on the body.

Our time in Albuquerque was beginning to end and Daddy was assigned to report for work in Minneapolis, Minnesota. Edith and I protested but we had to be with our parents. Not knowing the length of stay at Minneapolis, they decided to keep the Albuquerque apartment. We found Minneapolis and St. Paul very interesting. We both were sent to West High School as Edith was now in the 11th grade and I in the 10th. That experience was not like the previous one, but we did enjoy ice skating, attending a radio show, and other attractions that large cities can offer. I could not believe how cold it could get. Some days one had to dress in extra warm clothing just to be reasonably comfortable.

A labor organizer was not always welcome in some communities. Edith and I were instructed to never answer the door when our folks were not at home. They spoke of Daddy being followed home from work. We were never informed of much, but suddenly Daddy said that he did not care to be there. The three months ended abruptly and we were on our way back to Albuquerque.

Plans were being made for us to return to Denver the first of December. Daddy had some unfinished business that would take only a few days and Mother was busy getting things together.

It was on that Sunday morning, December 7, 1941, that Edith and I were playing on the grass embankment of the hospital across the street from our apartment when our parents shouted and waved to us to come in. Edith was fifteen and I was fourteen. The radio was turned on. The report was:

*Pearl Harbor, an inlet on the southern coast of Oahu near Honolulu, Hawaii, site of a United States naval base, has been attacked by Japan.*

Mother and Daddy were very upset. They were shocked and discussing the report with each other. Neither Edith nor I understood what was going on. We did not have much knowledge about Hawaii or why the Japanese were doing such a thing! We were aware that a terrible war was being fought in many foreign countries, but our country was not involved - yet.

Further news on the radio stated that the attack had started at 7:55 a.m. Hawaii time.

*The sneak attack was executed by about 360 planes from six Japanese carriers which, with two battleships, two heavy cruisers, eleven destroyers and miscellaneous other ships, comprised the Pearl Harbor striking force under Chuichi Nagumo. U.S. Pacific fleet units at Pearl Harbor comprised 70 combat vessels and 24 auxiliaries, most of them moored for the weekend. There were also about 300 U.S. Army, Navy and Marine Corps planes present. Of eight U.S. battleships in the harbor, five were sunk, one severely damaged and the other two hit. Two destroyers were also sunk and nine other ships sunk or severely damaged, which 140 aircraft were destroyed and approximately another 80 damaged. About 2,330 military personnel were killed and 1.115 wounded, and about 100 civilians were killed or wounded. The Pacific fleet's three aircraft carriers not at Pearl Harbor on December 7th escaped damage. The attack prompted the immediate entry of a vengeful United States into the war. (Encyclopaedia Britannica, 1965).*

Other later reports showed that 4,575 persons were killed, wounded, or missing. The day after the attack on Pearl Harbor, Congress, with only one dissenting vote, recognized the existence of a state of war between the United States and Japan, while Japan issued its overdue declaration of war against the United States and the British Empire. The Japanese sneak attack on Pearl Harbor was described as *a date which will live in infamy* by President of the United States Franklin Delano Roosevelt.

One of the ships, the USS Arizona, has a final resting place at Pearl Harbor where 1,177 crewmen lost their lives on December 7, 1941. A 184-foot-long memorial structure spans the mid-portion of the sunken battleship. There is a shrine room where the names of those killed on the Arizona are engraved on the marble wall. Oil has been coming to the surface from the USS Arizona since that fateful day at the rate of one gallon a day. It is expected to continue at that rate for another 100 years. The local Hawaiians refer to the oil seepage as the *Arizona tears*.

••••••••••••••••••••••••••••••••

World War II brought on many changes in our country. Patriotism ran rampant. It seemed as though every person wanted to help in some way. Edith and I were attending South High School in Denver and the boys in our classes wanted to enlist to be a part of the war effort. Some were not of age but their parents could sign permission for them to enlist if they were sixteen or older.

Volumes have been written about World War II. Personally, our family experienced many changes in the days and years ahead.

Since Daddy was recognized as a leading labor organizer in Colorado, a representative from the United States Navy approached him to enlist his service as a recruiter He thanked him for the offer but told him he was not interested. As so many men at that time wanted desperately to be in action defending their country in combat, this was not unusual. After Daddy and Mother did a lot of soul searching, she agreed that it was all right with her for him to enlist in the service. She knew how much it meant to him.

He was 39 years old when he enlisted in the Seabees (Construction Battalion) with the United States Navy on November 5, 1942. He was sent to Norfolk, Virginia for his basic training. Afterwards he returned to Denver and we all drove to California. He was stationed at Camp Pendleton as a Chief Carpenters Mate in the Third Marine Division. He and Mother rented a trailer on the beach at nearby Oceanside.

It was a pleasant stay at Oceanside as we all enjoyed swimming in the ocean and being together when Daddy could get a pass. We went to the base once and enjoyed attending a movie. While seated in the theatre there were two young Marines sitting behind us. They leaned over and whispered to Edith and me, "Get rid of the big guy." Daddy gave them a look that ended the conversation immediately!

A few weeks passed and Daddy received his orders. All he could tell us was that he would be sailing soon on a large ship to destinations in the South Pacific. He and Mother sold the car since the No. 5 streetcar was near our home in Denver and would be sufficient for our transportation.

Very sad farewells were said but we all knew that this was what Daddy wanted to do. Mother, Edith, and I returned home to Denver by train.

Letters were scarce from Daddy and we knew all too well that he was being kept busy fighting and helping with construction projects on islands in the South Pacific. When a letter did come it was usually limited on information since the servicemen could not write about details for security reasons.

In the meantime, Mother decided she would seek employment since Daddy's income was very limited while he was in the service.

She had heard that the Remington Arms Plant was hiring positions for work in their factory. Remington had received a commission to build a $52 million plant west of Denver in January of 1941. By the summer of 1943 the plant employed 19,500 workers. Mother was hired and took the streetcar across town to work. There was a shortage of men for a lot of jobs so they were anxious to hire more females. She could not tell us at that time what her work was for reasons of security. By August 1944, the ordinance plant was idle and Mother no longer worked for them. She later told us that her job was on a line with other women who made incendiary bullets. It was dangerous work. They had to wear special gloves and other attire to protect themselves. The pay had been very good and was a help to the family budget.

The news media in 1942 reported that the Third Marine Division had landed in Guadalcanal, the start of the first major allied offensive in the Pacific during World War II. We heard from Daddy later that he had been there; then his next landing at Bougainville in 1943. Guam in 1944 was the third invasion and where they repaired the shell-damaged seawall with native stone and cement. He was promoted to Chief Petty Officer in the Navy.

Attached is a picture showing the large net ladders that the troops used to descend into the landing crafts that took them to shore. Also, when they returned to the awaiting ship, they were used to ascend. This is when a terrible thing happened to Daddy. As he was pulling himself up the ladder he experienced such acute chest pain that he fell back into the landing craft and was unable to move. He had a massive heart attack.

After being airlifted to Hawaii, he was hospitalized in Oahu.

Mother was informed by letter and advised where Daddy would be taken. Shortly thereafter he was flown to Fitzsimons Army Hospital in Aurora, Colorado. There he recuperated for quite a while but continued to have additional heart attacks. He was discharged from the service on January 12, 1945.

Most servicemen did not like to talk about their war experiences and my father was no exception. When Mother questioned the markings on his legs he said it was jungle rot, a common condition for many. Some of the scars were from crab bites after they had dug their fox holes on the beach and tried to sleep at night. The sand crabs were relentless. The men had to keep pounding on the sides of their fox hole to deter them, but their legs were still bitten.

When I questioned survival in the jungles on those islands, he said that the "japs" hid in the high trees and shot the workmen. Also, a driver on a large CAT machine was an easy target. The enemy would take clothing from dead American soldiers and get in the chow line from time to time.

Words cannot describe the joy of having our family together once again. Daddy did not get to attend our high school graduations - one in 1943 and mine in 1944. He was far away, fighting a war that he thoroughly believed in and for his country which he deeply loved. We were all very proud of him.

In spite of Daddy's failing health he tried to keep active in his labor work and received the following award:

*United States of America Certificate of Award for meritorious service in the war effort is made to James W. Shirley in appreciation for your devotion to our country's needs expressed in your patriotic contribution of time and effort to the price control and rationing program. Dated 25th day of September in the year nineteen hundred and forty-five. Harry Truman, President of the United States.*

# Shirley Enlists In 'Seabees'

James Shirley, widely known Denver trade union leader who has been employed as organizer by Teamsters Joint Council No. 54 during the past two years, enlisted this week in the "Seabees," navy construction unit. He is now awaiting assignment.

The "Seabees" are men enlisted in the construction regiments of the navy who build the advance and mobile bases outside the continental limits of the United States. They are thoroly trained in military tactics and when assigned to duty are able to engage in combat, should the occasion arise.

*Newspaper articles about Shirley Enlists in 'Seabees'*

*James W. Shirley as Chief Carpenters Mate*

*Mary A. Shirley 1943*

Official U. S. Navy photogr[illegible]

*Amphibs hit Bougainville: The new landing-craft program means more and bigger actions of this type.*

[illegible] personnel [illegible] officers aboard landing [illegible] had experience in [illegible] and Asiatic operations, and [illegible] rated as competent, upon fur[illegible] training, to assume command of their own landing craft. Many of the officers will be former warrants of long experience; they will be given opportunities for amphib training and, if able to demonstrate their capabilities, will be given opportunities to command and a commensurate increase in rank.

Perhaps the largest source of new officers will be the midshipmen's schools —Columbia, Notre Dame, Northwestern—which will send most of their qualified graduates to one or another of the amphib bases. Practically all of these will be from the ranks of V-7. Beginning this month, considerable numbers of V-12's also become available for training.

These will for the most part be trained to become junior officers aboard LCs. If they prove their ability and rank commensurate with the positions they may be chosen to fill on the basis of their training [illegible] phibious Training [illegible]

Other, more matu[illegible] either have been on shore duty or who have had no prior indoctrination, will get an intensive course of training at the Naval Training School (Advanced), Ft. Schuyler, The Bronx, N. Y., studying seamanship, navigation, ordnance, gunnery and communications, in preparation for possible positions of command.

Nothing could be more indicative of the present attitude toward the amphibs than the fact that a large and mounting proportion of their officer personnel has accrued voluntarily. A recent estimate by those responsible for procuring personnel for this branch reveals that the proportion of midshipmen who put amphib training as their first choice has almost tripled. Now they look to it as a top source for action, and plenty of it.

A "rotational" policy of bringing of men who wer[illegible] ficers ab[illegible] L[illegible] [illegible] garde[illegible] [illegible] [illegible] of becon[illegible] COs of their own ships.

Engineering officers will be provided by Naval Training Schools, at Cornell, Penn State and North Carolina State, and still others will come from the General Motors Diesel school at Flint, Michigan, source of engineering officers not only for DEs but for LCIs and LSTs as well.

Communications officers will come largely from the Harvard NTS, where the last month of their four-month course will be devoted to special subjects in preparation for amphib work.

Although amphib training was originally pretty much of an Atlantic coast proposition—partly because the North African invasion was first on the list, and largely because the great sources of landing-craft construction were either Atlantic or middle West—amphib training is now a two-coast affair.

Italy . . .

Official U. S. Navy photographs
Bougainville . . .

Official U. S. Marine Corps photograph
Tarawa.

*Bougainville, November of 1943*

*Guam*

*James W. Shirley, Chief Petty Officer*

Sept 1945

# Colorado Federation Of Labor Picks Shirley

James Shirley, veterans' co-ordinator for the Colorado State Federation of Labor, was elected secretary-treasurer of the federation at the close of the 50th annual convention in City Auditorium.

Shirley, former business agent of the building trades unions, won by a considerable margin over George Maurer and Rudolph J. Cook. He fills a vacancy created by the resignation of James A. Brownlow, who has been appointed to a Washington post with the American Federation of Labor.

Shirley

George Brayfield, who was unopposed, was re-elected president of the federation.

Those elected vice presidents from the Denver district were Floyd Case, Ed Walsh, R. L. (Sam) Voorhees, William P. Schumacher and M. C. McDonough.

Eileen Major of Denver defeated Mary Rabnik for the post of vice president-at-large.

**Twenty-nine Resolutions Adopted**

Twenty-nine resolutions, covering a variety of subjects from rheumatic fever to independent unions, were adopted by the convention.

Among the more important resolutions brought in by a committee headed by R. L. Voorhees of Denver and adopted by the delegates were those:

1: Opposing "any form of military conscription."

2: Opposing return of the U. S. Employment Service to the states.

3: Urging support of legitimate consumer co-operatives.

4: Urging, in co-operation with the Chamber of Commerce, establishment of labor-management conciliation machinery.

**72-Hour Week Hit**

5: Calling on the state to pay overtime at standard rates to employes of the State Hospital for the Insane who are working a 72-hour week.

6: Indorsing the Wagner-Murray Full Employment Bill and condemning the Hatch-Burton-Ball Bill as anti-labor legislation.

7: Indorsing a minimum wage of 65 cents an hour with a proviso that a 75-cent minimum be reached within two years.

8: Calling for support of the Wagner-Ellender Bill, which is designed to provide a million new homes in the next 10 years.

9: Urging establishment of a permanent Fair Employment Practice Committee to combat discrimination because of race, creed or color.

10: Indorsing the proposed Missouri Valley Authority and calling for an educational campaign to inform labor on the merits of the proposal.

(By LESLIE SHOWERS.)

**AFTER angling for a crack at each other for several months, George Manley and Jim Shirley, Denver sockologists, have been matched for a decision bout. They will step twelve rounds in the stellar attraction of a ring card at Rawlins, Wyo., on Labor day. It will be Manley, the clever middleweight, versus Shirley, the hard-hitting light-heavyweight.**

F. W. Morgan, secretary of the Rawlins fire department, who is promoting the show, predicts a record crowd will turn out to witness the soiree.

Manley has a large following in Denver who are confident that he will dispose of Shirley in handy fashion. Shirley's admirers are singing the same song, but to a different tune.

Eaton, Colo., boasts of a promising middleweight. He is Harry Rogers, colored. Rogers claims to have defeated several southern 158-pounders including Kid Cash, Willie Mayfield, Jack White and Nat Dewey. He served in the ranks of Uncle Sam's fighting Yanks during the World war and while overseas qualified to box for the light-heavyweight championship by virtue of victories over Frenchmen Le Fevre and Boris.

Rogers is angling for a scrap with George Manley. He claims that he has been on the Denverite's tail for several months but so far has been unsuccessful in forcing Manley to engage in fistic combat with him.

Canon City fight bugs are all "het" up over the splendid showing their favorite, Kid Belt, made against Joe Burger at the latest stockyards stadium show. Belt was given a big hand upon his return to Canon City.

*Newspaper articles 1945*

United States of America

Certificate of Award

FROM THE

OFFICE OF PRICE ADMINISTRATION

THIS AWARD FOR MERITORIOUS SERVICE IN THE WAR EFFORT IS MADE TO

James Jr. Shirley

IN APPRECIATION OF YOUR DEVOTION TO OUR COUNTRY'S NEEDS EXPRESSED IN YOUR PATRIOTIC CONTRIBUTION OF TIME AND EFFORT TO THE PRICE CONTROL AND RATIONING PROGRAM

☆

Harry Truman
PRESIDENT OF THE UNITED STATES

Chester Bowles
ADMINISTRATOR

REGIONAL ADMINISTRATOR

DISTRICT DIRECTOR

DATED THIS 25th DAY OF September IN THE YEAR NINETEEN HUNDRED AND Forty-five

*USA Certificate of Award for Meritorious Service from the Office of Price Administration*

# Jobs Chief Concern Of Returning Service Men, Writes Shirley

When the members of the armed forces come back they are going to be looking for jobs, declared James W. Shirley, vice-president of the Colorado State Federation of Labor, who is now Chief Carpenter's Mate with the Seabees somewhere in the Pacific.

In a letter to S. W. Johnson, also a vice-president of the State Federation, Chief Shirley urged the labor movement to be on its toes "when this war is over and the boys start coming home."

James W. Shirley

A union will mean little or nothing to large numbers of them who have come into the service right out of school and never had jobs, he said, and they should come home to a well-planned program.

"You and I know what it means to have large numbers of unemployed; the men start bidding for jobs; they forget all about their unions—until they have large wrinkles in their bellies. Now is the time for labor leaders to give this matter much consideration, especially during the coming convention, when they are all together."

Chief Shirley expressed regret that he will miss the convention of the Colorado State Federation of Labor to be held in Denver June 23 and 24, but said he is pretty busy where he is. "Tell all the gang I said hello," his letter concluded.

*Newspaper article*

A highlight of his long career was when he was elected Secretary-Treasurer of the Colorado State Federation of Labor at the close of the 50th annual convention in City Auditorium in September of 1945. He introduced, supported, and shepherded twenty-nine Adopted Resolutions through the legislative process, a few of which are:

*Calling on the state to pay overtime at standard rates to employees of the State Hospital for the Insane who are working a 72-hour week.*

*Indorsing the Wagner-Murray Full Employment Bill and condemning the Hatch-Burton-Ball Bill as anti-labor legislation.*

*Indorsing a minimum wage of 65 cents an hour with a proviso that a 75-cent minimum be reached within two years.*

*Calling for support of the Wagner-Ellender Bill, which is designed to provide a million new homes in the next 10 years.*

*Urging establishment of a permanent Fair Employment Practice Committee to combat discrimination because of race, creed or color.*

*Indorsing the proposed Missouri Valley Authority and calling for an education campaign to inform labor on the merits of the proposal.*

With all his strength Daddy tried to continue his work but, after collapsing twice as he was speaking at meetings, he returned to Fitzsimons Hospital. Medical knowledge had not advanced sufficiently at that time for diseases of the heart and there was not much that could be done for him. Reluctantly, he had to resign his position and lead a life of rest with limited activity.

A year before his death, he and Mother made a trip to St. Petersburg, Florida. He was unable to join in activities but Mother enjoyed playing shuffle board. It brought back their memories of when they lived in Tent City and of Edith's birth there. Their "Florida Odyssey" was now their "Florida Paradise."

James W. Shirley passed away on May 23, 1962 having just turned to the age of 59. Labor never had a more devoted advocate and faithful servant.

He lived life to the fullest, served his family, friends and his country with all the passion and love that one heart could hold. For all who knew him he will ever be remembered as the *Hero of West Irvington Place.*

LABOR OMNIA VINCIT

CERTIFICATE

ORGANIZER

No. 12902

# American Federation of Labor

OFFICE OF PRESIDENT WILLIAM GREEN
A. F. OF L. BUILDING
WASHINGTON, D. C.

TO ALL WHOM IT MAY CONCERN:

**This is to Certify that**

J. W. SHIRLEY,

*is hereby duly authorized and legally commissioned to act as Organizer for* STATE OF COLORADO *with power and authority to found and install Local or Federal Labor Unions under the jurisdiction of the American Federation of Labor, to obligate and initiate members and install officers, in accordance with the laws of the National or International Union of the trade or calling of which the Union is composed, or if a Local Trade Union of which no National or International Union exists, or if a Federal Labor Union, then in accordance with the laws of the American Federation of Labor. It is the power, authority and the duty of the one holding this commission to aid in creating a greater demand for the products of union labor, union labelled products.*

**This Certificate** *to remain in full force and operation for one year from date unless revoked previous to the expiration of said term.*

**Given** *under my hand and seal of the American Federation of Labor this* 24th *day of* OCTOBER, 1947.

Wm Green

PRESIDENT, AMERICAN FEDERATION OF LABOR

*Certificate from American Federation of Labor certifying J.W. Shirley as Organizer for State of Colorado*

*DENVER SAID "HOWDY" TO CHEYENNE this week when its first postwar "booster party" to travel by air boarded a United Mainliner here and flew to the Wyoming capital to seek support of a move to bring assistant secretaries of four big government departments to the west to serve the Rocky Mountain Empire. Cheyenne looked on the idea with favor.*

*Newspaper article 1946*

*Union Officials broadcasting on KOA/KNBC Radio*

# EPILOGUE

Few people have the talent and ability to become true leaders. Some acquire leadership skills through the school of hard knocks and back-breaking labor; others combine their personal experiences with all of the above and rise to the top. Although the principle of leadership may be taught in the classroom, the true test comes when the pressure is on.

By giving this account, I have attempted to touch upon the time and events that shaped the life story of a unique and dynamic fighter, whether in the boxing ring or in the labor movement. James W. Shirley spent his adult life in pursuit of equality and justice. He had a deep and abiding love for his country, his family, and the people who spent their lives providing for their dependents by the sweat of their brows.

As a leader he could make things happen. His honesty and integrity seemed to draw others to him. He found his true calling in organized labor and spent much of his life fighting for those who could not fight for themselves.

As the daughter of this remarkable man I feel privileged to share these personal memories with you. Hopefully we can all stand just a little taller because he came our way.

**Doris Auger Davis,**
Author

# REFERENCES


*The Denver Post*
Newspaper, Denver, Colorado

*Rocky Mountain News*
Newspaper, Denver, Colorado

*The Colorado Gambler*
Monthly newspaper

*Aurora Public Library*
Aurora, Colorado

*Denver Public Library*
Reference Department, Denver, Colorado

*Colorado Historical Society*
Stephen H. Hart Library

*Encyclopaedia Britannica*
1965 Edition

*The American Heritage Dictionary of the English Language*
William Morris, Editor, 1969

*The Merriam-Webster Dictionary*
1997

*Out of the Depths*
by Barron B. Beshoar, Copyright 1942, 1957 Sponsored by Colorado Labor Historical Committee of the Denver Trades and Labor Assembly

*The American Nation*
by Hicks, Mowry and Burke, Fourth Edition, 1965 Copyright 1965, 1963, Houghton-Mifflin Company, Boston

*South Denver Saga*
by Phil Goodstein, Copyright 1991, Denver New Social Publications

*Trials and Triumphs*
by Stephen J. Leonard, Copyright 1993 by the University Press of Colorado

*Colorado in the Great Depression*
by James F. Wickens, Copyright 1979